Praise for *TIP*

"A team will only succeed, and a company will only grow, when each person on that team is responsible and accountable for their own results. If you want to consistently bring your best every day, you need to read this book and follow Dave's game plan for personal, team, and organizational success."

—Jon Gordon,
Wall Street Journal best-selling author,
The Energy Bus and *The Power of Positive Leadership*

"I love this story and this book. It truly sends a powerful message and takes what I have learned from Dave Gordon to the next level. I am sharing this with everyone I know and telling them to read it—*twice!*"

—Kurt Leisure,
Vice President, Risk Services, The Cheesecake Factory

"You cannot always impact what happens to you, but you always have the ability to respond. Dave Gordon is a master at helping you see through the fog of adversity and setting the right course for your future. He helps you discover your brand, and reminds you to always protect it."

—Jon McGavin,
Area General Manager, The Ritz-Carlton
and JW Marriott Orlando, Grand Lakes

"Every great athlete, CEO, leader, teacher, and parent understands that greatness is a journey filled with the creative meaning of trying, falling, crying, laughing—and persevering, because the journey is what makes the difference. In *TIP*, Dave uses the power of conversation, of words, to compel you to cheer the hero along, all the while really cheering for yourself to become the best you can become."

—Brian Hainline, MD,
NCAA Chief Medical Officer

"In a service industry, our employees are responsible for the fulfillment of our promise to our customers. Brand alignment, and the delivery of consistent quality customer service is crucial for everyone. In *TIP*, Dave has taken his "stand for your brand" principles we incorporate at Gallagher Bassett, and created a powerful resource with broad appeal and helpful guidance for any leader looking to build a world class team, company, or brand."

—Scott Hudson,
President and CEO, Gallagher Bassett

"*TIP* is a powerful personal and organizational vehicle for positive change. Management at all levels can use the book as an effective communication and organizational improvement tool that will lead to increased efficiency and productivity in their teams. The book can also be a positive and empowering catalyst for anyone who believes that his or her work, or personal life, should be more fulfilling."

—Doug Cain,
President and CEO, Unique Fabricating

"*TIP* is an engaging, wisdom-packed story that will help you take control of your life and career. Not the run-of-the-mill secret shortcut to success—Dave Gordon reminds us that "you have to be willing to do the work"—*TIP* illustrates simple yet powerful principles for discovering and building your authentic personal brand and taking personal responsibility for your success."

—David Mooney,
President and CEO, Alliant Credit Union

"After reading *TIP*, you will have no choice but to look at your own career and relationships through a different lens, one that empowers you to never accept being average, and to take control of your future with a simple plan for personal innovation."

—Jenny Hutt,
author, SiriusXM Host of *Just Jenny*, and co-founder of BunnyEyez

"*TIP* provides critical messages—in a quick, easy-to-read format—on leadership, and how to realize your personal and professional potential. Give more, get more . . . it's that simple. Help others be their BEST. Be of UNIQUE VALUE. Create WOW! This is a must-read at any stage of your life or career."

—JeMe Cioppa Mosca,
SVP, Rehabilitation, HSS—Hospital for Special Surgery

"*TIP* is an outstanding resource for young professionals or anyone hoping to advance their career. This book provides examples of best practices in personal accountability as well as keys to navigating and recognizing career laddering opportunities when presented at any age and stage of life."

—Kristen Lazalier,
Executive Director, External Relations, Michael F. Price College of Business, University of Oklahoma

"I'm always looking for new ways to motivate and inspire people to embrace the company culture and mission. This is truly a must-read for anyone in the hospitality industry, and should be reread every year as a reminder of the skills necessary to consistently deliver outstanding customer experiences. Dave, thanks for all the tips!"

—Tom Murphy,
CEO, West Side Hospitality Group

"How you feel about a brand or company often comes down to one individual who either cared deeply and took accountability for the experience of a customer, or just didn't give a flip. *TIP* is a resource for anyone who wants to inspire their people to care more and have a positive impact on the future of their career, the success of the company, and the strength of the entire brand."

—Ann Handley,
Wall Street Journal best-selling author of *Everybody Writes*, and Chief Content Officer of MarketingProfs.

A
SIMPLE STRATEGY
TO INSPIRE
HIGH PERFORMANCE
AND LASTING SUCCESS

TIP

DAVE GORDON

WILEY

Library of Congress Cataloging-in-Publication Data:

Names: Gordon, Dave (Motivational speaker), author.

Title: Tip : a simple strategy to inspire high performance and lasting success / Dave Gordon.

Description: Hoboken, NJ : John Wiley & Sons, Inc., [2020]

Identifiers: LCCN 2019031708 (print) | LCCN 2019031709 (ebook) | ISBN
   9781119641445 (hardback) | ISBN 9781119641490 (adobe pdf) | ISBN
   9781119641483 (epub)

Subjects: LCSH: Career development. | Success in business. | Success.

Classification: LCC HF5381 .G795 2020 (print) | LCC HF5381 (ebook) | DDC
   650.1—dc23

LC record available at https://lccn.loc.gov/2019031708

LC ebook record available at https://lccn.loc.gov/2019031709

Printed in the United States of America

F10016087_121120

For Kate, with all my love.
Because you know who you are.

CONTENTS

Present Day

FOREWORD

Thirteen years ago, when I published my first best-selling book, *The Energy Bus,* I thanked many people who helped me achieve my dream. Included in my acknowledgments was this paragraph to my brother, Dave:

> *Thank you to my brother for always challenging me and helping me improve this book. Your ideas, suggestions, and encouragement helped make this book the best it could be. I look forward to seeing your book next to mine in the bookstore.*

Well, the wait is over, and I'm so happy that my brother has finally turned his many years of industry leadership and creative expertise into his first book, destined to make a big impact on teams and organizations. Why am I so confident? Dave has spent his entire career building personal, team, and organizational brands, and *TIP* is the culmination of his life's work to date. A fantastic writer, an entertaining motivational speaker, and an inspiring leader and coach, Dave has crafted a game plan for your success.

Over the past 17 years, I've had the opportunity to speak to, and consult with, leaders of organizations, teams, and communities across the world. From NCAA champions to Super Bowl and World Series contenders, to the most highly respected and profitable Fortune 500 companies, there is one principle, when practiced well, that is consistent with high-performing teams and companies: personal accountability. A team will only succeed and a company will only grow when each person on that team is accountable for their own success and brings unique value to their role.

As my reputation and influence have grown as a speaker and author, I know the importance of consistency in words and actions when building a strong personal brand. Everything I do or say will have an effect on my life, my business, and the future of everyone around me. I am accountable for everyone close to me, so I live with one purpose: to create positive leaders, teams, and organizations, one person at a time.

After reading this book, and following Dave's guidance, you will see how your reputation and the recognition you receive in your career and your life are very much in your own control. You just have to remember who you are, what you stand for, and live with a driving purpose to help others be their best.

—Jon Gordon
Author of *The Power of Positive Leadership* and
The Energy Bus

ACKNOWLEDGMENTS

I want to thank the many people who have helped me in my life and my career. This book, and the goal of being a published author, could not be possible without the love and support of so many.

First and foremost, I thank my wife, Kate. You believed in me long before I believed in myself. My best friend, tireless editor, harshest critic, biggest cheerleader, and loving coach; this story has always been for you. Thank you for being the guiding and unwavering force of our home, our business, and our lives.

For my children, Dylan, Shannon, and Megan. Your input throughout the editing process for this book was invaluable. The three of you have been my inspiration. It has always been my goal to help you find your unique talents, and give you the support to discover your path to happiness and lasting success. Being your dad helped me discover mine.

For my brother, Jon. Thank you for encouraging me to find my purpose. I couldn't have done any of this without you.

Thank you to Shannon Vargo, Sally Baker, Peter Knox, Paul Dinovo, Vicki Adang, Deborah Schindlar, Matt Holt, and the team at John Wiley & Sons, for your guidance and expertise, every step of the way, as we brought this book to life.

To Scott Hudson for reading the book and sharing your suggestions to make it better. Your support and leadership continue to inspire me to always stand for my brand.

Thank you to my outstanding teammates at Gallagher and Gallagher Bassett. Every interaction is proof that a unique and thriving culture can be created and maintained for over 90 years, when you hire, coach, and train people who are aligned in a common purpose. #TheGallagherWay

To Kurt Leisure for sharing your risk management wisdom, and for *never not* being a representative of your brand.

To the leadership teams at The Ritz-Carlton Amelia Island and The Ritz-Carlton Orlando. I continue to share your stories of exceptional service, engagement, and customer experience.

To John Branciforte. Our conversation was a "wow" moment for me, and for this book.

To Katie O'Grady, my fellow outlaw. You were the first outsider I trusted with the book, and I thank you for your insights as a successful sales professional.

To Sheralyn Hartline and all of the nurses who bring their best to work every day. Your dedication to your patients and their families continues to amaze and inspire me to always give more.

Thank you to the many clients who have brought me into your companies and trusted me to speak, coach, train, and help inspire high performance, better communication, and personal accountability in your people and your teams. A special thank you to Lori Arndt for being one of the first, many years ago, to trust me with your business, and your brand.

To the meeting planners and executives who value my engaging style of visual, motivational keynote presentations. Thank you for choosing me to create memorable experiences for your most important audiences. It's what I love to do most.

To The Johns Hopkins University Writing Seminars Program. It's amazing where a great liberal arts education can take you.

I am also grateful for the authors and speakers that helped shape my career, and my business, with their words. As I think about this book one day sitting on someone's shelf or desk as a resource and guide to a better career, I look at the many books in my own office and feel blessed to have them standing at the ready when I need encouragement to be the best leader, speaker, coach, writer, and person I can be. I don't have personal relationships with most of these authors, but I want to thank them for sharing their expertise. Tom Peters, Pat Lencioni, Nancy Duarte, Ann Handley, Seth Godin, Dorie Clark, Dan Schawbel, Brené Brown, Daniel Pink, Carmine Gallo, Donald Miller, Jim Collins, John Medina, Michael Lewis, Malcolm Gladwell, Amy Cuddy, Randy Pausch, Mihaly Csikszentmihalyi, Theodor Seuss Geisel, Ken Blanchard, Spencer Johnson, and Jon Gordon. Thank you for sharing your secrets to success. Your work has inspired and influenced me in ways you'll never know.

Lastly, to my parents, Nancy and Joe. I miss you both, and wish you were here for just one more happy hour.

ABOUT THE AUTHOR

Dave Gordon is an internationally recognized brand, marketing, and communications expert. He is an inspirational speaker, author, coach, and leader on a mission to help people identify, communicate, and deliver their unique value to build stronger personal, team, and corporate brands. Dave's work has positively impacted leaders, teams, organizations, and associations in countries around the world, including the United States, Canada, the United Kingdom, Australia, and New Zealand.

Companies, teams, schools, and associations that have benefited from Dave's involvement include: The Ritz-Carlton, Marriott International, American Express, Novartis, PwC, Arthur J. Gallagher & Company, AutoZone, Gallagher Bassett, Alliant Credit Union, Southern Glazers Wine and Spirits, Samsung, Hospital for Special Surgery, Apple, Twin Peaks Restaurants, Quanta Services, VF Outlet, Manpower Group, Whole Foods, Oklahoma University—Price College of Business, Baylor University Center for Professional Selling, and the National Retail and Restaurant Defense Association.

Dave is the co-founder of Gordon Creative, a brand alignment and communications consultancy. He is also the Chief Marketing Officer of Gallagher Bassett, the premier global provider of risk and claims management services, dedicated to helping people face adversity and uncertain futures with confidence. Dave is a graduate of The Johns Hopkins University. He's not a doctor, but he did play one on TV.

Dave invites you to visit at www.davegordon.net, follow on Twitter and Instagram @davegordon_9, or connect on LinkedIn.

Introduction

Your reputation is the most important asset in your career and your life. When nurtured and managed correctly, it can bring you limitless and lasting success. When ignored, you allow others to define your value, and control your future.

I was compelled to write *TIP* to help people who desire a simple way to take charge of their careers, improve their performance, manage their reputations, and enhance their lives.

TIP is for the professionals and high potentials who want a resource and a plan to help them make a name for themselves as valued stand-out performers for their teams and organizations.

TIP is for leaders, managers, and coaches who want to inspire their people and improve the productivity of their teams. *TIP* creates a common language of expectations and value, on which you can build stronger relationships and better results.

TIP is for young professionals and the next generation of talent entering the workforce who need a guide and a plan to build their career of a lifetime.

TIP is for anyone in any stage of work or life who needs the inspiration to remember, or discover, their passion for what is most important. You always have the power to create a new beginning for your own story.

Lastly, *TIP* is for my kids, and anyone who wants to help their kids have a positive future. In a world where we are judged by every word and every action, we must be strategic in how we promote ourselves today, and protect our reputations for tomorrow. *TIP* allowed me to have those conversations with my kids and encourage them to make the best decisions for lasting success. I hope it helps you to do the same.

*   *   *

I believe in "infotainment." We learn better when we are not bored. We remember more when we are entertained and engaged. As the late *Last Lecture* author and professor Randy Pausch said, "Don't tell people how to live their lives. Tell stories. They'll figure it out for themselves."

Rather than a typical how-to book, *TIP* is a story and a strategy written to remind people in any position judged by performance that the only way to achieve high performance, and lasting success, is to consistently take accountability for your reputation and your results.

Based on personal experiences and the lessons I've learned as a C-level executive, brand strategist, communications coach, sales leader, motivational speaker, performance trainer, bartender, actor, husband, and father, *TIP* is meant to engage you as only a story can. It is also meant to help you remember that the lasting success you desire is dependent on one thing. You.

Your thoughts. Your words. Your actions. And the value you create.

I believe everyone has value. You are not put on this earth unless you are meant to bring value to another person, community, team, or organization. When you do the work and give everything you've got, you will be valued greatly and rewarded in return.

TIP is my story, not just because I wrote it, but because in many ways, I lived it. It's a business story, but it's also a story about second chances, redemption, reinvention, and love. When you love what makes you unique, and discover what you truly stand for, it's much easier to acknowledge your purpose and value in this world. And when you know your value, every word, action, and decision in work and life becomes so much easier. You pick a career you love, surround yourself with the right people, and create the best situations to help you achieve the results, recognition, and reputation you deserve.

Enjoy the story, and most importantly, follow the strategy.

It really works.

1 The Biggest Day

Brian Davis was like most people. He did some of his best thinking in the shower. Yet, today, all Brian could think about as the water hit the back of his neck was which underwear he was going to wear to work.

Black?

It's strong. Black makes a statement, even if no one can see it.

But, Brian was going to wear the blue suit, so maybe blue to match the suit. Although, matching the suit was not the intention. It was the tie that really mattered.

Yes, this was the biggest day of his career and his life. So, why was he focusing on his underwear instead of the real decision that was about to take place, that would affect so many things in his life?

Brian stepped out of the shower, wrapped the towel around his waist, and began shaving his face as his wife, Jen, came into the bathroom.

"Suit, shirts, and ties are on the bed," she said as she grabbed her hairbrush.

"I'm thinking black at this point," Brian replied.

"Uh-huh," she answered.

After 24 years of marriage, she knew him better than he knew himself.

"You don't think so? You think blue?" he asked.

"Brian, you have agonized over your colors every big day of your career. I love you with all my heart, but don't drive me nuts before you even have all your clothes on."

"This is the biggest day. You know that."

"I know," she said.

"I need all the good vibes I can get today. It's a big day for all of us."

"Right, and wearing the right colors will send the forces your way. I understand."

"You're mocking me," he said.

"I would never do that to the potential future CEO of a *Forbes* five-star luxury brand," she smiled.

Brian smiled back at her. She was still playful and sarcastic. She challenged him in all the right ways.

"Finish shaving, do that thing with your hair I always like, and meet me in the bedroom. We'll help you like we always do."

"Thank you," Brian smiled.

Maybe the color thing was his way of not dealing with the stress of the meeting, or the pitch, or the promotions he faced throughout his life. Maybe it was his way of maintaining control of what was about to change.

Brian finished shaving and walked into the bedroom. There, laid out on the king-size bed were the choices. Jen was standing with her arms outstretched in her best *Price Is Right* pose.

"Kids!!!" she yelled, "color time!!!"

It was a fun ritual when the kids were young. When they started it, the kids were just six, four, and two. Jen read that including them in decisions around the house would improve their self-esteem. Having them help their father pick out his "colors" for the big days was fun for everyone. And majority vote always won. That way everyone had a chance to be part of the good fortune if and when it happened. After 12 years, the kids still had an unblemished record.

Which is why at ages 18, 16, and 14, Brian strongly encouraged them to continue helping to pick the "big day colors." Couldn't stop a good thing. Superstitious? Maybe. But, more importantly, Brian knew it really annoyed them.

"This is getting ridiculous," said 18-year-old Drew as he dragged himself into the room. "I've got a paper I'm trying to finish before school."

"Tell us again why we have to pick out your clothes for you. If my friends knew about this . . .," said 16-year-old Sara.

"For good luck," Jen interjected.

"Blue," said 14-year-old Kyra.

Drew rolled his eyes.

"She always picks blue, 'cause it's your brand . . . whatever . . . fine," said Sara.

Drew nodded.

"Okay. Blue it is. Thank you for your help everyone," Brian said as the three kids shot out of the room.

Brian looked at Jen. "That was fun."

"Always is," she laughed.

"So, blue?" he said, holding the blue tie against the blue suit.

"Yes," she nodded, "Yes. This one goes with your eyes, which are very blue today. And it has been your go-to color all along. Trust yourself."

Brian did trust himself. He had put in many years of hard work and dedication. But so had the other candidates who were up for the position. They all worked hard, and some had twice the tenure with the company that he did. They all put in long hours at the office, traveled internationally, and always took their jobs home with them. The hardest part of the whole situation was the fact that they could all do the job, but only one would eventually run the global organization. They were all friendly, but to call them friends would not be entirely true. They were colleagues. However, they all respected one another, and each of them knew the decision would not be based on who was least deserving. It would be based on who was the best choice for the future of the organization.

So, what was it that was going to sway the decision in his favor? What quality or little something was going to convince the current CEO, and the board of directors, that he was the one who should be trusted with the future of the company? When the talent is that even, the decisions always come down to the little things. The final decision usually rests on a feeling or an instinct. Emotion. Brian kept wondering, had he done enough?

He tightened the blue tie around his neck, gave it a final tug, looked at the dog, who was watching him from across the room, and proclaimed himself ready. The dog seemed impressed, but she chewed her own feet, so how much could he really count on her? He threw his suit jacket over his arm and headed down the stairs into the kitchen where Jen was having a cup of coffee.

"Anything going today?" Brian asked as he poured himself a cup.

"I have a buyer for the building on Third Avenue," she replied.

He nodded.

Jen continued, "Drew's got track practice till 6:30. Sara is studying at the library with the girl we can't stand, but how much trouble can she get into at the library? Never mind . . . don't answer that. And, Kyra is going shopping with me for dinner. We'll all meet back home by 7:30 and whatever happens, we will all be together."

Brian smiled at the thought.

"All three kids with us, eating together, at the same time?"

Jen smiled back and gave him a hug.

"Let's just say that when it comes to special moments in life, I want to make it an experience," she said.

"I like the way you think, Mrs. Davis."

"Thought you might. If I'm not mistaken, you did remind me of the same kind of thing a while back. Now go out there and bring us home a CEO for dinner. And remember that no matter what happens, we love you. At least I do. I'm not really sure about the kids."

Brian chuckled as he gave her a kiss goodbye. He maintained a smile as he turned to head out the door, not wanting to let on that deep inside, he was as nervous as he had ever been in his life. Win or lose, his life was going to change. Everyone around him was going to be affected.

He called goodbye to the kids as he walked out the door and got into his car.

Had he done enough? He would soon find out.

2 The TIP Jar

As Brian made his way up the elevator and through the offices on the 36th floor, he tried to shake off the nervous energy he was feeling. Anytime there is a shake-up at the top of the organizational chart, there are bound to be changes that ripple throughout the company. One decision. Many changes.

After getting to his office and listening to a few voicemails of "good luck" and well wishes while scrolling through the e-mails of the same nature from people who were aware that this was decision day, he finally stopped and clicked open the e-mail labeled *TIP*.

TIP

What's in Your TIP Jar?

If it's overflowing with tips and you gave everything you could, then luck and well wishes aren't necessary. Take pride in who you are, the way you communicate, your actions, and the unique value you bring every day. Remember all the people you have helped along the way. Whatever happens today is part of the plan.

Brian smiled. He looked at the glass jar sitting on the edge of his desk. At that very moment, the nervous feeling disappeared. All of the wasted worrying stopped. The pressure he put on himself to carry the load for others stopped. The thought of failure stopped.

He stared at the glass jar and started to remember a time when he was at another kind of crossroads in his life, when he could have just as easily not taken his current path. He wondered what would have happened to him, his family, and all the people he helped along the way. What if he hadn't been in that place 12 years earlier, at that moment? What if he hadn't gotten the wake-up call he needed to become more accountable for his own success?

Brian picked up the glass jar and held it in his hands, recalling the moment when his life was going in a very different direction.

Twelve Years Earlier . . .

3 A New Direction

"**Y**ou know, Bri-man . . . I think you're a great guy, right?" The slurring words came out of Chris Conroy's mouth.

"And I really hate to be the one to tell you, but since you're a great guy and all, I can't let you walk in there tomorrow without knowing."

Brian stared intently at his director of sales.

"The company is moving in a new direction, and unfortunately, they're going to be letting you go. Word has it that it's going to be about 10 from sales. I'm really sorry to be the one to tell you, but I thought you should know."

Brian tried to remain composed.

"What the hell are you talking about?" he stammered.

Chris Conroy just shrugged.

"Can't tell you much more than that. I just heard that a RIF is happening and 20% of the entire company is being let go."

"RIF?" Brian asked.

"Reduction in force. Company is in the red, and the higher-ups need to see profits in order to be attractive to potential buyers. So, they're tightening their belts and letting go of anyone not considered valuable to the new direction."

Brian wanted to ask Chris so many questions. Why him? What new direction? What did he mean? Brian had never missed a quota in 10 years. Did they realize at 39 years old he had a wife and three kids to support? The knot in his stomach tightened, and he had the overwhelming urge to throw up.

"What do you mean, a new direction?" was all Brian could ask.

"Not sure what they mean," slurred Chris. "All I know is, the big cheese is sending out an e-mail tomorrow, and if you're on the list, you're gone. The little cutie from HR who has a crush on me told me you were on the list. We're supposed to have this conversation tomorrow after you get your e-mail, but I just thought you should know now . . ."

"Are you on the list too?"

Chris hesitated. "Umm. Well, no."

"So, what is this . . . a farewell drink? Is that it? Is that why you took me out tonight?" Brian's voice was getting louder. "Firing me in a public place so I wouldn't react?"

"I'm sorry. I really think you're a great guy. But the numbers just weren't there. It was really close though. Quota unfortunately was the bottom of the scale . . . the minimum."

Before Brian could respond, the bartender came over and stood in front of the two men.

"Seems to be getting a little loud in here for a Tuesday night. Everything okay?" he asked.

"Everything's fine," Brian answered. "Just fine."

"Good," the bartender responded. "Can I get you guys anything else?"

"No . . . actually I have to go," said Chris. "Not feeling too good."

Chris slid off the bar stool and quickly grabbed his bag and coat. He gave Brian a quick pat on the back, as if to say goodbye, it will all be okay, no hard feelings, and please don't hate me, all at the same time.

"Just put it on your expense account," he slurred. "I'll okay it when it comes in."

Brian didn't even look up as Chris headed out the door.

What was he going to do? Was he really going to be fired? Maybe Chris got his info mixed up and he really wasn't on the list. His mind began to run through every possible scenario of what the next day was going to look like. He imagined it all a mistake. He imagined how he was going to look and act as he read the computer screen telling him to get his stuff out of the building. Would they really fire people by e-mail? Brian imagined how he would get revenge. He'd find a way to shut the damn company down. He didn't know how, but he would. He was angry . . . confused . . . furious! But, he had no one to direct that anger towards now that Chris had left the bar.

The bartender walked back over after taking care of the couple at the end of the bar and once again stood in front of Brian.

"Your friend have a little too much to drink?" he asked.

"You could say that," Brian responded.

"Looked like a little more than that, though. You guys were getting a little heated. Seriously, is everything okay?"

"No, not really."

Brian paused.

"I'll take another beer when you get a chance."

The bartender grabbed a beer out of the cooler and popped the cap with his silver bottle opener. He placed it in front of Brian and then waited.

Brian paused for a few seconds and then let it out.

"That guy said I am about to be fired tomorrow morning. He said I'm on a list of people who are being let go. I'm not sure if he's right or wrong, but being that he's my manager, I don't think he'd tell me if it wasn't true."

The bartender stared at him for a moment before he responded.

"I'm Jack, by the way."

"Hey Jack . . . Brian." He gave the bartender a half-hearted handshake.

"Nice to meet you, Brian. Welcome to Crossroads. Look, whatever is going to happen is going to happen, so you can't dwell on the possibilities, unless there is something you can do about it. I have a philosophy about moments like this. Want to hear it?"

"To be honest, Jack, not really. Philosophies are great in theory, but if you were the one being fired, I think you'd be singing a different tune."

Jack nodded. "I'll get you the check, then."

Jack the bartender went to the register and rang up the final tally.

Jeez. The guy couldn't even pay the check when he knew I was being fired the next day, Brian thought. "I'll okay the expense when it comes in." Damn right you will.

Jack put the final bill on the bar.

"Last round was on me," he said, "sorry about the bad news."

"Thanks."

Brian opened up the bifold containing the bill and saw a tab for 35 dollars. He did the calculation in his head. What should he tip? Normal service is 15%. Good service is 20%. It was good service. 20% would be seven bucks. Brian filled out the tip, signed the check, and put it back on the bar. As he gathered his things, Jack came over and said thank you before even opening the bifold. As he walked back to the register and opened the booklet to ring the tip amount into the register, he stopped and turned quickly around to face Brian.

"$35 tip. That's 100%," he said.

"Yup."

"Thanks so much. I really appreciate it."

"Not a problem," said Brian as he picked up his computer bag, "Chris can explain that one to the finance department when I'm not there."

"Listen," said Jack, "could I get your business card? I do an e-mail newsletter, letting people know when we are having specials and things like that here at the bar. Plus, I write about things once in a while that you might find interesting."

Brian pulled out his business card and tossed it on the bar.

"Won't be worth much after tomorrow, so feel free to send whatever you want. A virus would be nice."

Brian decided he would not tell Jen until he knew for sure. Seeing how it was only one day away, or more like 12 hours to be exact, why give her an extra amount of worry in her life? The only thing worse than getting fired, Brian thought, was the rumor that you are about to be fired.

Brian got into a cab and headed for home. Tomorrow, Brian thought, would be a very long day.

4 Dear Valued Employee

Brian got up early and arrived at work at 7:30 a.m., anxious to see what the day had in store for him. He wanted to make sure that all of the personal files on his laptop were copied, just in case his departure was immediate. There were no illegal files or things he would need to hide from the company, but he did have a few folders like poems to his wife, a few funny stories he had written for the kids while on the commute back and forth to work. These folders along with everything else would be deleted from the computer, and the laptop would just be issued to someone else. Just like that. Was he really that replaceable? "Quota was the minimum," Chris had said.

As Brian turned on the computer, he wondered how many people would log on to their own computers and see the e-mail. Would they expect it? Did they have a manager give them the heads up already, or would it come as a complete surprise? He was guessing most would be surprised. Brian did a Google of "RIF" and "fired over e-mail" which turned up a few hits including an article in *BusinessWeek* about a president of a company who fired 400 people over e-mail. Thoughts of his tenth-grade girlfriend breaking up with him over the phone popped into his head. Coward.

He looked around his small office. Pictures of the kids and Jen everywhere. Inspirational quotes tacked up all over the room. His favorite being from Albert Einstein, who said, "If you are of value to your friends, family, clients, and community, then you truly are a success." He didn't know how successful he would feel today if he were fired. At that point, how much value would he be to anyone. How much would he be worth?

Precisely at 9:15 a.m. the e-mail from the company president hit his inbox.

There it was, in the subject header line, in bold letters, "Thank you for your service."

Thank you for your service

Dear Valued Employee—

It is with regret that I must tell you that our organization is in a restructuring phase. Unfortunately, we are eliminating your position, as it is no longer in line with the new direction of our company. We feel it best to let you pursue other opportunities now, rather than later, when all of these changes are finalized.

Thank you for your time of service to our organization. We wish you good luck in all your future endeavors.

Best Wishes,

Matthew Harrison

P.S. Your manager or supervisor will speak to you about your severance package and the necessary steps you need to take before leaving the premises today.

Nope. Brian corrected himself. The rumor of being fired is not worse than being fired. And what made it worse was Chris already told him, so he couldn't even have a genuine freak-out session. Brian was so emotionally drained from thinking about being fired that when it actually happened, all he could do was let out a big sigh. Dear valued employee. If he were so valued, why was he getting fired? Corporate doubletalk. He didn't even want to burn the building down anymore, or call the fire department to report violations in safety codes, or go into the supply closet and take a lifetime worth of pens and a few bags of the cheap coffee from the breakroom. All he wanted to do now was get all of his stuff and get out.

He clicked open the e-mail from his manager that arrived right after Harrison's and saw the document that said Brian was to receive a 10-week severance package upon termination. One week for each year of service. What a horrible word. Termination. Terminated. Hasta la vista, baby.

Brian then read that he was to leave his computer in his office, hand in any outstanding project work to his manager, and vacate the building with all of his belongings. Ten years of loyalty with the same company and this is how it ends. With an e-mail and a kick out the door.

Just then, Brian heard someone crying down the hall. He poked his head out of his office to see people telling each other that it would be okay, that everything happens for a reason, and there is always a light at the end of the tunnel and that they would be there for each other, and all the other meaningless platitudes people say in these situations.

This wasn't the way life was supposed to happen. You don't get fired for being loyal. You don't get fired for making quota. You don't get fired when you have a family of five to feed and clothe. When you and your wife have decided that she will stay home and raise the kids, and you will work because you have great job security and she wants to spend time with the kids while they're young. It's just not supposed to happen that way when you are already making sacrifices for the greater good in life. So, if it wasn't supposed to happen, why was it happening?

After he shut his door, he went back to his desk and put his head in his hands. Brian's eyes began to well up with tears. He couldn't believe at 39 years of age he would have to go out and try to find a new job. Would anyone even hire him? Was he too experienced or not experienced enough? He had friends in sales who were still looking for jobs almost a year after getting fired. How could this have happened? What made him so expendable after all his time and effort?

"Damn it!!"

Brian grabbed a napkin that was sitting on his desk and dried his eyes. He wasn't sure how much time he had to get his stuff together before he would be escorted out of the building. He went back to the computer and continued to copy his personal files. In the meantime, he checked the rest of his e-mail to make sure nothing important was missed before he was gone.

There was an additional e-mail from Chris Conroy titled, "Sorry." Brian deleted it before even opening it. There were e-mails from people working on current projects, most likely looking for answers that only Brian would be able to provide. He deleted those as well without opening them. They would have to find out the answers themselves. Maybe they would find out how valuable he really was. Or, then again, maybe he wasn't. He began to question everything he had done the past 10 years.

As his files copied, he continued to delete e-mails, until he came to the last one titled "TIP" from Jack the bartender. Maybe it was the virus Brian had asked for. He clicked it open.

TIP

Dear Brian:

I believe people come into your life for a reason, a purpose. Some are there to give you something, and others come to receive.

TIP is the title of an e-mail newsletter that I send out to friends and customers. A TIP is something you can give, but also get. Being so close to my customers, just about three feet away, allows me the chance to see life in a different way. So, from time to time I share observations that are personal, professional, and always universal.

You said to me last night that I would be singing a different tune if I was the one about to be fired. Well, I wrote the e-mail below a long time ago, but I think you will appreciate it today. I hope you don't need it and that you still have your job. But, if not, please allow me to share my experience as someone who has been where you are now.

YOU'RE FIRED

I worked in the same place for close to five years. After working an entire weekend on an important project, I was called into the new manager's office first thing

Monday morning. He proceeded to tell me that it was time for the department to make a change, that they were going in a different direction and my services were no longer needed. "We're going to have to let you go," he said in a very business-like manner.

Five years of my life in a job that was a part of my identity. A place I shared defining moments of my life. Many successes and failures along the way. No longer needed. I would have to start over.

There comes a time in everyone's life when someone more powerful than you decides that you have no value to them anymore. For whatever reason, real or fabricated, that person has the ability to shake up your world and change everything. Their perception suddenly becomes your reality.

It's not just your job. It could be a friendship, a love, a marriage, or even a family relationship. It doesn't matter, because when you are on the receiving end of being let go, it hurts. It cuts to the core of who you are. At that moment you can do one of two things: you can cry about how you are no longer needed and begin to question your own value, or you can believe that somewhere out there, someone needs your services. Someone else wants the unique talents that only you can bring.

People who self-destruct after being fired do so because they are looking at themselves through the eyes of the person who fired them. They start to question themselves. They lose their confidence and, ultimately, continue through life scared, waiting for someone else to drop the hammer on them. They stop living and just start surviving.

But the people who get fired and bounce back are the ones with resilience, who know they have real value in their world, and whether it's a job, a love, a family, or a friendship, those people know there will be others who will want their services. There will be others who will appreciate that special something that they have to offer. Many times, it turns out to be even better than the situation they were in.

You are the hero in your story, and heroes always bounce back. Choose to be resilient. The rest will follow.

Take It Personally,

Jack

Brian read the last line over and over again. For the first time all day, he smiled. He thought of his kids who would come running and jump into his arms when he walked in the door from work.

Brian would not look at his world through the eyes of his president, or his manager, or his co-workers saying how sorry they were to see him go. Brian would look at his world through the eyes of his family and those he loved, and those that loved him. He would take control of his own life. He had 10 weeks of severance to find another place where he would be respected and valued. But, Brian realized, only if he valued himself first.

5 First Impressions

Two weeks after Brian was escorted out of the building he had called home for 10 years, he found himself back at the bar called Crossroads.

Brian walked in and found a seat in the middle of the bar. He was looking for Jack, but instead there was a pretty woman with long dark hair behind the bar. It was fairly busy for a Wednesday happy hour, and Brian had to wait about five minutes before she could get to him.

"Hi," she said. "What can I get you?"

"How about a Corona?" he responded.

She grabbed a Corona out of the cooler and popped the top.

"Do you want to run a tab?" she asked.

"Umm, no thanks. I won't be staying long. Just wanted to stop by and see the bartender, Jack. Is he working tonight?"

"He is, but not coming in till later. And he's not just the bartender. He owns the place. If you can hang around, he'll probably be in at eight."

"Actually, no, I have to get home. I just wanted to thank him for something."

Brian took a swig of the beer.

"Did he send you a TIP?" she asked.

He nodded.

"Thought so, that's what people usually thank him for. Either that or it's a sarcastic thank you for getting them plowed until they can't see straight. Which one did he send you?"

"You're fired."

"Never saw that one."

"Well, I guess he sent it because I was actually fired."

"Sorry to hear that," she said.

"Thank you," he responded. "I had an interview in the area today which went okay, but I've got a really good interview tomorrow, which is why I can't hang around tonight. I wanted to thank him for giving me something to hold on to. Changed my perspective, if you know what I mean."

"I know exactly what you mean," she said. "See that guy over there?" She pointed to a well-dressed man talking to a group of other well-dressed men and women who looked like they just walked off the cover of a Brooks Brothers catalog. "That guy was a waiter here three years ago. Now he owns his own catering company. Used to talk to Jack all the time about wanting to own his own business."

"See that woman over there?" The bartender pointed to a woman sitting at a table near the back of the bar. She was talking with a group of other women, and they were all laughing. "She's been one of Jack's followers since he started his newsletter. They've all been followers. They all come in to see him, and they always bring big crowds with them. Which is why I love working for him. There's always a crowd. And that means big tips for me. By the way, that woman is one of the partners at the biggest law firm in the city. When she met Jack, she was basically a functioning alcoholic on the verge of failing out of law school."

Brian turned back around to face the bartender.

"I'm Brian," he extended his hand.

"Kelly," said the pretty brunette with the beauty mark on her right cheek. "Nice to meet you."

Chris Conroy was the one who suggested they come in for that final drink. Brian had never been in this bar before that night, even though it was close to his office. Correction. His former office. The best way Brian would describe the bar would be upscale comfortable. Cushioned bar stools spaced nicely across the length of the long mahogany bar. Tables for groups to gather or eat at the far end, and a few couches towards the back in a lounge area. The music playing added to the energy, but it could barely be heard over the many conversations taking place. Maybe that was why it felt so comfortable. People were engaging with one another. They were enjoying each other's company, having what seemed to be important conversations.

"So, since you can't hang around, do you want me to leave Jack a message?"

Brian grabbed a napkin off the bar and wrote down his personal e-mail address.

"Tell him this is my new e-mail address, and he can send me whatever he wants. Also, tell him I'm the one singing a different tune. He'll know what it means."

"Will do," she said as she put the napkin in a cup by the register.

Brian walked out of the bar. He stood on the sidewalk and turned back to face the building. He looked up at the bright blue and red Crossroads sign hanging over the doorway. Brian had a feeling he'd be back.

6 The Offer

Two more weeks had passed when Brian once again walked into Crossroads. It was a Tuesday happy hour, so every seat at the bar was filled except one towards the middle. He immediately grabbed it and sat down.

"Well, look what the cat dragged in . . ." Jack immediately came over to him and extended his hand. "You had an interview, a couple of weeks ago, right?"

"Right," Brian answered.

"Well?" Jack fired back after a short uncomfortable pause.

"Well . . . I didn't get it." Brian's shoulders slumped forward. "They said it was a tough decision. That I was very qualified, but ultimately the deciding factor between me and another finalist were the intangibles. A gut feeling like the other person would fit in better."

"What do you mean?" Jack asked.

Brian took a deep breath.

"I had prepared all my answers about where I went to school, team sports, work to date at my last job to show my ability to work in a team environment, my job experience to date . . . even that weird question they always ask about 'what is your biggest weakness?' I was prepared."

Jack nodded.

"The interview was going great. And then the interviewer asked me if I had any questions."

"And what did you say?"

"Well, I asked how much the job paid, how many weeks vacation we got, what kind of office would I be in. Stuff like that. I wanted to make it seem like I was already there. You know, like already part of the company."

"Hmm . . . ," Jack stroked his chin.

"When I got the call and asked the woman why I didn't get it, she said that I would be good at the job, but she needed a self-starter. Someone who wanted more than just a paycheck."

Jack reached into the cooler in front of him and pulled out a beer. He held it up to Brian.

Brian shook his head. "Nah, just a club soda would be fine."

Jack filled the glass with ice and then filled the glass with soda from the beverage gun. He put it in front of Brian, said, "Be right back," and then raced down the bar to take care of the couple that just walked in the door.

Brian watched him greet the man with a firm handshake and then lean way over the bar to give the woman a quick peck on the cheek. Obviously regulars. He had so many of them. It was like they were all coming over to visit him in his living room.

When he came back a few moments later, Brian was slowly twirling his straw in his glass.

"What would you have changed if you could do it all over again?" Jack asked.

"To tell you the truth, I still would want to know what I asked. I might ask the woman if she liked working there or something like that, but ultimately I can't think of what else I would have asked at that moment."

"Did you ask about the company?"

Brian thought for a moment. "A little, but not in detail."

"Is that because you already did the research on them and knew the answers?"

"I went to their website. Did some research on them . . . enough to know I could see myself working there. It was a friend of a buddy from college who got me the interview. I knew he liked the company. It was a somewhat easy product to sell. That was good enough for me."

Jack stared at Brian.

"But were you really curious about the company . . . what they did . . . how they made a difference in one way or another. Why they were in business? Did they give to the community? What was it really like to work there? Are there company softball games? What is the culture like? What is the timetable for advancement? How is your performance measured, and who will be evaluating you?"

Brian raised his eyebrows.

"Brian, you were so worried about coming home with the job so your wife and the kids would give you the big hug and kiss and do the 'Daddy is great' dance, that you forgot why you were there. You forgot why that company was looking to hire you."

"And why is that?" Brian leaned forward.

"So you can make their company better. So you can add value to their culture. Did you read their mission statement before you went in? Their credo?"

Brian stared blankly at Jack.

"You were already thinking about your money, your vacations, your office. WIIFM. What's in it for me, instead of what you could do for the company and how you could make a difference. That's what your interviewer wanted to hear. An interviewer wants to hear what you will bring to the company. Not just what you did in the past but how you will enhance the future of their place. Your questions are always a good indication of your intentions."

Brian knew Jack was right, but he was more interested in the quantity of his interviews instead of the quality. Sales. Law of averages. Something will stick if you put yourself out there enough.

"I'm smarter than that," Brian said. "I would want to make a difference."

"Truthfully?" Jack asked.

"Yes. Truthfully."

"You just lost your job. You're worried about how to pay the mortgage, the doctor bills, and new clothing for your kids. Plus, you have to eat. Did you really care what that company did? Did you really care if they sold dog food, airplanes, or cocktail napkins?"

Jack was right. He didn't care. He wanted a decent paying job. He would worry about a "career" at another time. Right now, he did have bills to pay, and the thought of doing anything would be okay as long as he had a roof over his head and some savings in the bank. He slowly nodded.

"You're right," Brian gave in. "I didn't care. Just wanted to get a new job and come home to my family to let them know everything would be okay."

"So, that said, let's take it back a little further. Why do you think you lost your job?" Jack asked.

"I don't know. I was making my quota."

"By how much?"

Brian gave an acknowledging shrug and put his thumb and index finger very close together.

"By the skin of my teeth."

"So you were doing what they asked you to do. But no more . . . no less."

"Yup."

"Average."

"Yup."

"So, I guess it would be fair to say that when a company sets a quota, what they are really saying is . . ."

"Quota is the minimum." Brian interrupted. He got it.

Jack took Brian's glass and refilled it with club soda. He handed it back to him.

"Listen. You lost your job because someone somewhere decided that you weren't holding up your end of the bargain. You may have thought you were successful based on meeting quota and all. But, from their perspective it could have been like you said, this is the bare minimum we expect. And, perspective is reality, so the person in charge . . . well, that person's perspective is everyone's reality."

"That's for sure."

"Anyone can be average. That's why they call it average."

Jack ran his hand through his hair, and then rubbed the day-old scruff on his chin.

"Listen, I have an idea," Jack said. "Turns out the guy who is our third bartender on the busy nights is getting married and will be away for about 10 weeks. Extended honeymoon with some business mixed in while they are in Europe. He's a musician, so he's here and there most of the time. Great bartender, so I keep bringing him back when he's in town, but I figure, you could use the cash, and I can use a body to help out."

"Me . . . bartend?"

"Yes . . . you . . . bartend."

Brian laughed out loud.

"I have trouble mixing milk into my coffee. You looking to shut the place down or something?"

"Look, I'm not saying you're going to run the place. That's my job. We just need a body to help out. We put all the tips into one bucket at the end of the night. and we split every-thing evenly. Cash in your pocket. And it leaves you free to job hunt during the day. You'll work Friday and Saturday nights, and maybe a Sunday once in a while. Plenty of time to recover if you schedule your interviews Monday through Thursday. And I can guarantee that you will learn a lot more than just how to make a margarita."

"My dad used to call me a bull in a china shop," Brian chuckled.

"Be sure to wear a pair of black jeans and comfortable shoes or black sneakers."

"But . . ."

"See you tomorrow night."

"I . . ."

"4:00 p.m. . . . just in time to set up for happy hour."

Then it hit him. Brian said he would dig ditches, clean up garbage, flip burgers if he had to. Here was a guy handing him a job he was not qualified to do. No one else was banging down the door. Cash. Time to find his next job during the day. Make the severance last a little longer. He said okay and went home.

That night, Brian woke up at 2:00 a.m. He couldn't remember what he was dreaming about, but he knew he was standing on top of a bar and he wasn't wearing any clothes. People were laughing. He was going to make a complete fool of himself. He'd be better off digging ditches.

That's when he decided to write Jack and let him know it wasn't going to work out. He would make up something. Sick kid. Yeah, that always worked when he needed a day off at the office.

Brian turned on the computer and opened up his e-mail.

Another TIP.

TIP

To all my friends—

As you know, Jimmy is getting married soon and will not be at Crossroads for a while. So, to pick up the slack, we have a real rookie joining us. His name is Brian and he, like many of you, is in the corporate world. He's between jobs and was kind enough to agree to help us out for the next 10 weeks. When you get the chance, please come by on a Friday or Saturday and introduce yourself. Even better, tell him your own story of transition and transformation. In honor of our rookie who might still be asking why I picked him to join us, please see below.

Take It Personally,

Jack

CHARACTER IN A CRISIS

I was talking with a regular customer one night, and I asked how her relationship was going with her new boyfriend. She took a deep breath and told me that he wasn't the person she thought he was. She suddenly had a health problem, and he was nowhere to be found. Worse, once he found out, he made it into an inconvenience for him. How dare she even expect him to change around his very busy schedule.

I once learned from a writer friend that you could learn a lot by taking all of the characters in your story and imagine them seated around the same table. On that table is a bottle of red wine. At a given moment, the bottle will spill and each of the characters will react. One will lead the cleanup, one will jump away so as not to get a stain on their new designer outfit, one will cry, one will scream at the injustice of such a waste, one will blame at least one other person for doing it . . . and so on. You may not even know how your characters will react until you really think about the crisis of the spill. You may even discover something new about one of them that you never would have believed. Wine leaves a stain, just like the most difficult and challenging moments in our lives.

Character is who you are and what you do when no one else is looking. And even further, according to my writer friend, true character is character in a crisis situation. I have seen and caused my share of spills and mistakes. I have learned something about myself, and others, in those minor crisis situations. Some people like to yell and scream for the attention of being wronged. Others like to make a scene and demand justice, or at least a free round. Some just want to clean it up and get on with whatever they were doing. Still others don't even seem to care as long as you make it right. A little club soda for the stain, and everything is fine.

We all have our share of spills and mistakes in our lives. That's what makes us human. But how we react to those spills, and how others react, should say something about who we are and those with whom we choose to surround ourselves.

Did you ever think you knew someone until you saw him or her in a crisis situation? Did they behave the way you thought they would? Maybe they disappointed you because they weren't exactly what you needed at that time. Maybe you thought they would be the one to run away, and instead they stood strong. You can't hide true character in a crisis. That is when real heroes are willing to step in and clean up the mess.

So, the next time you are questioning someone's true character, wait for the spill and see what happens. You may be surprised by their reaction, and your own.

Take It Personally,

Jack

Brian shook his head. Hmm, sick kid. Guess that seemed silly now.

Brian deleted the e-mail he was going to send to Jack and then shut down the computer and walked back upstairs. He made the rounds checking in on all the kids peacefully sleeping. Then he climbed back into bed and closed his eyes.

Time to clean up the mess.

7 New Beginnings

Brian walked into Crossroads and headed back to the bathroom to change his shirt into the Crossroads uniform. A black T-shirt with a stylistic typeface spelling CROSSROADS across the front. On the back was a drawing of a man and a woman standing at an intersection with their hands on their hips looking up at a road sign with four arrows pointing in different directions.

He made his way back to the front of the place and crossed through the waitress station and went behind the bar. Jack gave him a towel.

"Brian, you have to remember that the best bars are microcosms of the world. You get all walks of life in a bar. From the richest of the rich to the homeless person who just scrounged a dollar for a happy hour beer. No one is better than the other. Once you learn to serve each one with the same respect and thoughtfulness, once you learn to talk with each person in their language, only then will you truly be a good bartender, a good business partner, and quite frankly, a better person. It's the main reason I left my corporate job and opened this place. I was tired of answering to a boss, a company, and a brand I couldn't support. So, I scrounged every dollar out of my savings. Borrowed from anyone who would back me and opened this place. I call the shots. Literally. It could be many years before I own the place outright, but that doesn't matter. I'm not here to get rich. I'm here to serve."

Jack gave Brian a big pat on the back.

"Before we open the doors, I just need to show you a few things so you can function back here. Remember, Kelly and I are here to help, so if you have any questions, just ask."

Jack quickly showed him how to use the register for the evening, where all the bottles were set up behind the bar, where all the beer was located in the coolers, and the menus for when people wanted a specialty cocktail or something to eat. Jack showed him the proper way to wash the glasses, where the backup bottles were, in case they ran out, and how to pop a bottle top with a bartender's church key bottle opener. He showed Brian which button on the beverage gun corresponded to which beverage . . . C for cola, G for ginger ale, etc., the proper way to make a few of the most popular basic drinks and shots, and ultimately which glasses were for particular drinks.

Kelly came down from her side of the bar and pointed to her watch.

"We've already got a crowd lined up," she said.

"Kelly has the point . . . that's the front of the bar . . . and, Brian, if you know what's good for you, stay out of Kelly's way. I'll take the service bar to take care of the waitresses at this end of the bar, and you've got the middle. Kelly and I will try to float down and help you whenever we can, but now you know the basics, so you should be okay. Friday night is mostly a beer, wine, and shots crowd anyway."

Brian nodded again. That's all he was doing, nodding. He felt like one of those bobblehead dolls in the back of a car.

"All right," Jack declared, "let's open the doors!"

Kelly was right. It was the busiest Friday night Crossroads had experienced in a long time. Besides the 15 people that immediately came in the bar, a going-away party of 30 co-workers walked in the door unannounced 10 minutes later. In addition to the regular Friday happy hour crowd celebrating the end of yet another grueling hard-fought week of work, 20 people from the financial district came in to celebrate a highly successful day of trading. Needless to say, everyone there was ready to celebrate something, even if it was just the fact that they wouldn't be working for the next two days.

By the end of happy hour at 7:00 p.m., the bar was completely full. Jack was serving the waitresses and control-ling the music, making sure the playlist was matching the energy of the crowd. They were all moving at maximum speed to accommodate all of the customers' requests, as well as the waitresses who were serving the tables. It was controlled chaos.

In the middle of it all was Brian. Over 300 people, three-deep at the bar, and everyone wanted something. By unofficial estimates, in the first three hours Brian had broken four wine glasses and two highballs, chipped five shot glasses, and smashed an entire bottle of cheap vodka.

At first, Brian actually thought he was doing well. But then people wanted more than one thing at a time, and within an hour, a good drink was anything that didn't end up all over the bar, himself, or the customer.

Every so often, Brian would look over at Jack, who seemed like he had eight arms going at once, filling glasses, pouring liquor, popping beer bottles, going into the register, and counting money. He was amazing.

Kelly was the same. In fact, Brian thought she was even faster than Jack. How the hell was he going to keep up?

"You okay?!" Jack yelled over the blaring music.

"NO!" Brian screamed back. "HELP!"

Brian had at least 10 people screaming in his face and waving money at him, shouting their drink orders.

"Pick one," Jack yelled as he was popping the caps off eight beer bottles in rapid succession. "Just focus on one order at a time. You can't do it all at once. Drown out all the others for the moment. Pick one. You're in charge. You choose who is most important. Remember, your perception is their reality. You're in charge now."

Brian pointed to a guy in a blue sports jacket holding a twenty in his hand.

"Three Buds!" the guy shouted.

Brian grabbed three beers, handed them to the guy, took the money, made change, and handed it back. The guy left two dollars on the bar, which Brian quickly picked up and put in the tip bucket.

"Three shots of tequila and three Heinekens," a woman with too much jewelry called out.

Pick one. Drown out the others. Eventually you'll get to all of them. You're in charge, he thought, as he poured the shots.

As people left the bar, others started coming in. Brian felt a little better focusing on one customer at a time, but he was still pitifully slow, and everyone knew it. He was so slow that the customers were leaving him cheap tips, or not tipping him at all.

Midnight came, and by this time Brian's arms were sore. His back was starting to get stiff due to all of the bending. He couldn't remember being on his feet for that long, ever. He was sweating as if he'd just spent an hour in a sauna, and he smelled like a bar. As the hours passed, he kept wondering what had he gotten himself into?

8 What Is a TIP?

Brian watched as the last person walked out of the bar at 4:00 a.m. The evening was over. He made it, although he felt and looked like roadkill.

Jack and Kelly had begun to clean the bar as the crowd started to thin, so when the last person left, they only needed to wipe down the bottles and count out the registers.

It was about 4:30 a.m. when the three of them finally sat down at a table along the back wall of the lounge area. It was the first time Brian had sat down in 11 hours, and he felt as if a knife were sticking in the lower part of his back. *Totally out of shape*, he thought, as he rubbed his eyes.

"So," Jack said pointing to the three tip buckets on the table, "good night?"

"Yeah, I think so," said Kelly.

"I'm just glad it's over," added Brian. "That was probably one of the hardest things I have ever done. I don't know how you guys do it night after night."

Jack flipped over all three of the tip buckets, and Brian watched three mounds of money spread across the table. They all started unfolding and stacking the money into piles. There were some fives and tens and a few twenties here and there.

As they continued to count, Jack spoke.

"You know Brian, Kelly and I weren't born back here. We didn't come out of the womb with a bottle opener in our hand. We started at this at one time or another, and I won't speak for Kelly . . . but when I started, I wasn't very good at it."

"Like me . . . ," Brian added.

"No, not as bad as you," Kelly added, "I've never seen anyone break more glasses in one night than you. But you did manage to keep the glass out of the ice, so that's a good thing."

"I saw you really trying to keep up. That is the first sign that you are going to do well. You cared about what was happening, and that's a very important thing to remember. That's really the essence of customer service. People will forgive poor service from time to time, if they know you care about them and want to give them a good experience."

Kelly continued to pile the dollar bills, wrapping stacks of a hundred with rubber bands.

"The true differentiator in business is service. Products can be replicated or copied so, nowadays, it's really about the experience someone has when they interact with you. Someone can go anywhere for a vodka tonic or a glass of wine. Why do they come to me, and why do they come back for another one? Somehow, I'm providing a unique experience they might not get anywhere else."

Jack held up a stack of the singles.

"Do you know what the term TIP stands for, Brian?" Jack asked.

Brian shook his head. "Not really. I know what it is, but not what it stands for."

"Many people think TIP is an acronym for 'to insure promptness' or 'to insure performance.' It's supposed to guarantee someone will do a good job because if they don't, they aren't going to get paid as much if the service is bad. A tip is supposed to put the control of the experience in the hands of the customer. As you know, it's very popular in the service and hospitality industries, places like hotels, restaurants, and bars."

"Makes sense," Brian added. "If I put a tip cup on my desk and everyone gave me a dollar each time I did something for them, I might still have my job."

"I look at tips differently," Jack added. "If the thought of someone holding a dollar over my head is the reason I'm going to do a good job, that's external motivation. No one ever succeeded at anything meaningful in this world being motivated externally. My definition of TIP is different. I believe that TIP stands for **Take It Personally.** You see it on my e-mails. A tip is not what you get. It's what you give. It's what you give of yourself. If you are motivated internally instead of externally, your success in life is going to be exponentially greater. Do the work, give all you have, and you will be rewarded in return. I know that there are going to be some people who don't tip, no matter how good my service is. But I can't worry about them. I have to focus on the majority of the people who will see my value because I have taken care of them in a way that no one else ever has. And I can only do that if I take every interaction personally. If I do it right, they leave here, and they're going to tell all their friends to come to Crossroads because they had an amazing experience, because of me. When I go home and look in the mirror and know I did all I could for my customer, I will have a level of satisfaction that is not determined by the money in my pocket. That satisfaction comes from taking everything I do personally."

Brian nodded.

"If we always identify ourselves based on our salary or our job title, we are doomed to one day be very disappointed in ourselves when that title is gone or our salary is cut. We have to identify ourselves on our own terms, or others will do it for us. When you go home tonight, think about that. Think about how you were perceived at your last job. Ask yourself this question: At my last job I was valuable to who . . . And then fill in the blank with as many people as you can, and describe the value you brought to them."

Kelly finished splitting up the tips and handed Brian's share to him.

"Pretty good night," Kelly said turning to Brian. "Imagine what we could all do together when you actually know what you're doing back here."

Brian took the wad of cash wrapped in a rubber band and shook both of their hands.

"Are you sure you want to split this equally?" he asked. "You guys did so much more of the work."

"Yes. Keep it. Brian, before you go home I want you to think about something. Tonight you filled a role back here. You were average."

"Below average," Kelly inserted.

Jack gave her a look that said, give the guy a break.

"She's right . . . below average, but it was your first day," Jack added.

"A drunk monkey could have broken fewer glasses and made more tips," she added.

Jack ignored her comment and turned his attention to Brian.

"Your value was picking up the slack, which allowed Kelly and me to do our jobs and not have to worry about sliding to the middle of the bar. You were a placeholder. You filled a need, and let's face it: we could have probably put anyone in your shoes tonight to do the same job. I disagree about the monkey comment. I think you did better than a monkey might have, but truthfully, if you didn't come back tomorrow, no one would miss you."

"So, I assume you were never a motivational speaker in a previous life," Brian said.

"Listen, I'm not saying that to be mean. If you went to school for this and spent four years working at this and still weren't very good, that would be different. This was your first try at something new. We all made money tonight, but we might have been able to make more if you were better."

"If Jimmy was here we would have done about 30% more," Kelly added.

"Now, Brian, think what that guy who fired you with the e-mail thought when he saw your numbers compared to the top performers. What if, in his mind, he's thinking about what business would be like if he could get 30% more out of your position. He already knows after 10 years that he won't get it out of you. You were a placeholder. You filled a role and a need. But when budgets get tightened and performance gets looked at closely, there is no way to hide in the tall grass anymore. Last month, and tonight, you were exposed as the weak link. Would you agree?"

Brian nodded.

"Go home and think about your value. When you come back tomorrow, we are going to talk about doing a few things differently. For the next bunch of weeks we are going to expose you to a different mindset as it relates to how you look at yourself, your career, and your future. You are going to learn to TIP."

"And, while we're helping him with his mindset, can we do something about the broken glasses?" Kelly asked.

"Sounds like a plan," Brian said. He shook hands with Jack, and Kelly gave him a fist bump as he made his way towards the door.

That night, or technically that morning at 6:00 a.m., as Brian finally put his head on the pillow, his mind was still spinning. Brian replayed every drink he made, every conversation he had, and every glass he broke. His kids would be up in about an hour, and Brian knew he had to get some sleep, but he couldn't stop the thoughts.

When was the last time Brian left work and actually thought about work? No wonder he was fired. It was rare he was in the office after 5:00 p.m., and even when someone needed his help, Brian reluctantly gave it. If Brian had been making more of a contribution to the company, he wouldn't have been fired. If he had volunteered to do things that would make a difference, they would never have even thought to let him go. If he thought more about just the paycheck and the bills, he might have been considered valuable to the company. They would have begged him to stay. Brian thought about what Jack said. At my last job I was valuable to . . . whom? Being honest with himself, Brian tried to fill in the blank, and at that point he couldn't deny his lack of value.

Brian shook his head to try to shake the thoughts out of his mind. Sleep. Must sleep. As he tossed onto his side, he was able to stare at Jen, peacefully sleeping. How lucky he was to be with someone so loving, caring, and inspiring. He wouldn't let her down.

Even though she was sleeping, he gently put his hand on hers and whispered, "I will make you proud of me again."

Jen opened her eyes and smiled at him.

"You already do . . ."

He smiled back, softly kissed her, and then eventually fell into a deep sleep.

9 Wake-Up Call

It was noon before Brian woke up. He did not hear any sounds in the house. No screaming, no banging of doors, no giggling. As he got out of bed and walked downstairs he realized that he was alone. He couldn't remember the last time he was alone in the house. Brian usually left before anyone in the morning and usually was the last to get home at night. On the weekends, they were always together. It felt strange being by himself in the middle of the day. He made his way into the kitchen and saw the note from Jen next to the wad of money he left on the counter from the night before.

> *We went to your sister's house so the kids could play with their cousins. Thought you could use the extra sleep, since you'll be working again tonight. Can't believe you made that much cash in one night. Maybe you should just bartend the rest of your life. ☺ Enjoy some time to yourself. Love, us. P.S. there's coffee in the machine. Just hit the button.*

Brian made himself the coffee and a couple of fried eggs. He also took a few Advil since his back was a mess and his knees felt like the second day after the annual Thanksgiving family Turkey Bowl football game. He could barely raise his arms over his head. But he liked the feeling. It was a good hurt, as his college coach used to say. It was a hurt that reminded you that you were involved in something worthwhile, and you gave it your all. The thought of going back to Crossroads in five hours already exhausted him, but he looked at the money and felt lucky to have the opportunity for the extra income while he searched for a new job. His severance would only last another six weeks.

After he put his plate in the sink and poured himself another cup of coffee, he went over to the computer.

Brian sent his resume to a bunch of companies via a few online recruiting sites, so when he clicked open his e-mail Brian was hoping to see an invitation for a conversation or an interview. He knew being a bartender forever was not in his future.

Nope. No responses.

But, there was a TIP and it was sent at 6 a.m. Unbelievable, Brian thought. Does this guy ever sleep?

He opened the e-mail.

TIP

Hey Brian—
     Thought you should know that I was not trying to make you feel bad about your internal and external motivation last night. I'm glad you decided to take my offer and join us at Crossroads. I know you will be putting your name out there for interviews at new

companies, but just remember it can take a while to secure a face-to-face with a hiring manager. In the meantime, you have a few months with us, and I don't care how many glasses you break.

What I'm trying to say is, slow down. Think about what you really want out of life. Sometimes we think we have to keep moving as fast as possible to stay ahead, when in reality it's the times we pause and think that allow us to reach our goals. I wrote this when I was still a rookie behind the bar. I think it holds true today.

GLASS IN THE ICE

No, not ice in the glass . . . glass in the ice.

There are those moments on a Friday night behind the bar when everything happens in a blur. From the moment I walk in the door and take off my jacket, someone is screaming for a drink, an extra napkin, change, more liquor, more juice, an extra-long straw. I figure on a good night, I can make over two thousand drinks. At that point I'm running on autopilot. I have no concept of time. No concept of the world around me, except for the eyes glaring in my direction and the money being waved to get my attention. It doesn't stop until someone yells, "Last Call!"

Unless there's glass in the ice. When a glass breaks anywhere near the ice bin, the whole world stops. It has to. It's not like you can ignore it, because you or the other bartender can accidentally serve someone a drink with broken glass in it. The world stops. And the amazing part is, people understand. They realize they won't be able to get a drink until all the ice is dumped out, the bin is cleaned, and finally filled with new ice. Then the chaos can resume.

There are "glass in the ice" moments in all of our lives. Usually it's funerals, car accidents, a sick child. They are all moments when even though the world has you moving at the speed of light, everything less important must stop. And the amazing thing is, everyone understands. That big meeting has to be postponed. Your dinner date is canceled. The boss offers to console you instead of fire you. No questions asked.

So, I have an issue with glass in the ice. Why is it only bad things that make people understand and empathize? Why can't you walk into work one day and say, "I was late because my daughter wanted to draw me a picture and give me a hug before I left the house. I missed the train. Sorry, but it was really important to her."

Sometimes, when the world is screaming for another something, take a big glass and smash it in your own ice and tell everyone, "Sorry, gotta change the ice. You'll just have to wait a moment." If you do that from day one in any new job or any new relationship, people may realize what's most important to you. If you slow down long enough, you may even figure it out yourself.

Take It Personally,

Jack

Brian thought about his broken glasses and not hitting the ice at all the previous night. He thought about the jobs he applied for online and all the other job sites and headhunting services. He was just looking for a job. Any job. Maybe he needed to pause for a moment and remember what mattered most to him. He had been selling products and services since he graduated college. Maybe he was meant to do something different. Or maybe he was meant to sell something he actually believed in.

At that moment Jen and the kids walked in the door. They were all whispering, but it was a really loud child whisper that is actually louder than regular talking. He didn't mind as he already finished his second cup of coffee. When they saw that Brian was awake, they all ran over and gave him a screaming hug.

"The bear is awake!" they all yelled.

Brian looked at Jen. "The bear?"

"Yes, that's what we are calling you when you need to sleep in from working so late. We say, shhh . . . don't wake the bear."

Sara gritted her teeth. "GRRRRRR!!!!!"

Brian growled back.

"Well, you all did really great this morning. I didn't hear a thing!"

"Hey, Dad," Drew chimed in, "can you watch TV with me?"

"Me too!" shouted Sara and Kyra.

Brian smiled. He thought about the work he should be doing and the companies he should be researching for his next job. But, once he thought about "the ice," the decision of what was most important at that moment was easy.

10 Labels and Purpose

Brian showed up at Crossroads at 6:00 p.m. The night wouldn't start getting busy until around 8:00 or 9:00 on a Saturday, but Jack said getting there early was probably a good idea to get more familiar with his surroundings and his products. Also, if he showed up early, Kelly would show up around 8:00, and Brian would actually be able to leave early if the crowd died down before closing time.

Even though he had two cups of coffee at home, Brian made a quick stop at Starbucks near the bar and picked up a grande coffee with two extra shots of espresso. He had a feeling he would need it.

Jack was already behind the bar. He was still in prep mode, cutting lemons and limes, and there were a few customers quietly nursing their drinks and watching the game on the TV screens high on the front wall of the bar.

"Mr. Davis," Jack said as Brian walked in, "I am so glad to see you. Kelly bet me 20 bucks you would call in sick today, so I just got a bit richer without making a single drink."

"Well, glad I could help," Brian laughed.

Jack wiped his hands on his towel and shook Brian's hand from across the bar.

"Before you come back here for the night, have a seat. I told you that you would learn more than just how to make a drink back here, so let's talk about your brand."

"My what?"

"First question. What's a brand?" Jack asked.

Brian looked at him quizzically.

"Umm. Well, a brand is a name, you know like a name brand."

"Good. What else?"

Brian thought a bit more. "It's an identity. Image?"

Jack took Brian's Starbucks cup and put it on the back bar and replaced it with a coffee cup that was obviously from the deli down the street. It was blue and had a picture of a steaming cup of coffee on it and read, COFFEE.

"Is this a brand?"

Jack looked at the blue coffee cup.

"No. It's coffee."

"Would you drink it?" Jack asked.

"Sure, if it was the only coffee there was to drink, I guess so. I need my caffeine."

Jack brought Brian's Starbucks cup back and placed it next to the blue cup.

"Okay, now you have a choice. What do you pick?"

"I pick mine. The Starbucks."

"Why?"

"Because I know what I'm getting. Your cup of coffee could have come from anywhere. It could taste horrible. There's no label. I don't know how it will taste."

Jack reached into the cooler and pulled out four beers. In front of Brian, side by side, he put a Bud Lite, a Coors Lite, and a Miller Lite. Next to the Miller Lite he placed a beer bottle with no label.

"Which one do you pick?" Jack asked.

"What's in the bottle with no label?" Brian asked.

"I don't know."

"Well, I know I'm not picking that one."

"Why?"

"I have no idea what it is, or what I'm getting."

"So, which one?" Jack asked.

"They're all basically the same to me," Brian said.

"But you have to pick one."

"Okay. I pick the one on the left."

"Why?"

"'Cause you don't have Corona up there."

"Corona is a dollar more."

"I'd still pick Corona."

"Why?"

"I like it . . . and it was the first beer my wife and I ever had together on our first date. So, it reminds me of that. It's worth a dollar more to me."

"So, would you say you have an emotional connection to your beer?" Jack asked.

"That's kind of a weird way to put it, but yeah, I guess so."

Jack put the beers back in the cooler.

"That is a brand. When people are willing to pay more for a name, knowing they will get something of value, that's a strong brand. Think about the cereal you buy for your kids, the detergent you use to clean your clothes, the car you drive, the soap you use. They are all brands, and chances are you pay more for them than you would for a lesser-known or generic brand. You have relationships with your favorite brands. You actually seek those brands when you are in the marketplace and don't even see any other options."

He paused for a second to let it sink in for Brian.

"There is a reason why companies spend so much time and energy and money on branding their products and services and, quite frankly, the companies themselves. Have you ever heard of decision fatigue?"

Brian took a sip of his coffee. "No. Can't say I have."

"Decision fatigue is something we all face every single day of our lives. We make decisions from the time we wake up in the morning to the time we go to bed at night. We spend so much time making decisions that when we have the opportunity to not have to worry about making a decision, we take it! We actually crave it."

"I know what you mean. I used to come home and my wife would ask what I wanted for dinner, and I was so tired I really couldn't think. I literally could not make one more choice."

"Exactly. That's decision fatigue. And that's how brands become part of your life. You trust the brand to deliver exactly what you believe it will, without having to think about it. There is a promise of value the brand offers, and since you believe the promise based on past experiences, and an emotional connection, you keep buying because the brand doesn't let you down. You become brand loyal. The brand understands you have a rough life and decisions should be easy. That's why they call those decisions no-brainers. No more thinking necessary. Great brands become trusted partners, even collaborators in our lives. We form relationships with them even if they are nothing more than a label or logo on a coffee cup."

"Makes sense. What corporate thing did you do before you owned a bar?"

"I was a brand strategist. I'd help organizations create and align their brands. I learned a lot, and helped companies get more productive, but now I like to focus more on people." Jack paused. "Speaking of people, what's a personal brand?"

"Well, I guess it's basically the same thing as branding for products, but for people," Brian said.

"Exactly. Your personal brand is what makes you unique and what you are best known for. It's your reputation and so much more. So, if I said Volvo, what word immediately comes into your mind?"

"Safety."

"Bingo. If I said Steve Jobs?"

"Innovation."

"Yes. Albert Einstein?"

"Brilliant," Brian replied.

"So, in the same way you remember a brand for one thing, strong personal brands are also remembered by most people for one thing. Make sense?"

"Sure," Brian answered.

"And, here's the thing . . . most people don't really see themselves being known or famous for something. So, they go through life and do their jobs and make a living, but they are not really being guided by any plan or purpose. They are not celebrities or famous athletes, so they don't think about themselves as a brand. But personal branding is using the talents you have to promote yourself in a way that is less about 'look at me' and more about educating others on the value you can bring to their world, so they don't have to think about it when they need someone with your talents. No-brainer."

Brian finished his coffee and gave the empty cup to Jack to toss into the garbage behind the bar.

"So, what are you known for?" Jack asked.

"Me?"

"Yes, in one word, what are you known for? What do people say about you when you leave the room? Because when all is said and done, that is your personal brand. You can say anything you want about yourself, but it's what others say about you when you are not around that ends up being the true value of who you are."

"Ummm . . ." Brian was stumped.

"Did you have time last night to think about who would consider you valuable to them at your last job?"

"Yes. I now know why I was fired."

"No value?"

"Not much."

"So, what were you known for?"

"Trying."

"Trying?"

"Yeah. Whenever my boss would ask about getting my numbers up, I would always say I was trying. I was trying but not always succeeding because I probably wasn't trying my hardest. So, I was labeled Tryin' Brian. I believe it was more sarcastic than endearing."

Jack turned around to the back bar and grabbed three bottles of wine. He put them in front of Brian.

"What do these labels mean to you?"

"Not much, I don't know any of these wines."

"Have you ever taken clients out for dinner in your previous sales roles?"

"Of course."

"And, when it was time to pick out the wine, which would you choose?" Jack asked.

"Not the cheapest and not the most expensive. Something in the middle," Brian answered.

"Something new, or something you knew?"

"Definitely something I knew. I wanted to seem knowledgeable to my client."

"So, you picked the label you were familiar with . . . the brand you knew."

"Definitely. I would never take a chance on a wine that I knew nothing about. If for some reason the client hated it, the dinner could be ruined and might even cost me the account."

Jack put the wine bottles back on the back bar.

"Brian, that is exactly why, from this day forward, you need to look at yourself as a brand. When the world knows who you are and what you stand for, your brand becomes more known, and it's easier for people to pick you. They won't ever be disappointed because they know what to expect as long as you deliver on your reputation. You, just like any product or company, have a unique promise of value to anyone who comes in contact with you. So, I'm going to introduce you to the concept of thinking of yourself not just as a person with a job or a career. I'm going to show you how to build and maintain a strong personal brand that will help you succeed beyond your self-imposed limitations. You are about to have 10 weeks of new experiences that I guarantee will change the perception of who you are and what you are capable of. We are all the sum of our experiences and our decisions. It's all of these experiences, that will affect how people perceive your label."

At that moment a woman in her early thirties came up next to Brian and slid a business card in front of him.

"Did I hear someone say label?" she asked.

Jack immediately reached over the bar and gave her a hug.

"Brian, meet Tracy. As you can see from her card, she is the super premium representative for the distributor that supplies us with all our wine and liquor."

"Brian, very nice to meet you. I read about you from Jack's TIP e-mail. Welcome."

Brian shook her hand. "Nice to meet you as well. Super premium?"

"Super premium," she added.

"Sounds important," he added. "What do you do?"

Jack laughed. "I am so glad you asked that question, Brian. Do you remember when I asked what do you want to be known for?"

Brian nodded.

"Well, Tracy first sat across from me about, what was it, three years ago?"

Tracy nodded. "Yes. It was my first month on the job, and you asked what I did. And I said I am a sales rep for a wine and liquor company."

"And what did I tell you?"

"You said that answer put me into a group with about 20,000 other people. You said just by the way I described myself I was decreasing my value. You said if I didn't have something specific to be known for, then I was just in a group of people who were identified by either their job title or job function. And, if I continued to do that, I would always be a commodity without unique value."

Jack nodded. "Brian, what does her card say?"

Brian picked up the business card. "Tracy Wilson. Super Premium Business Partner, Wine & Spirits."

Jack smiled. "Tracy, what do you do?"

Tracy took a breath and spoke as if she had rehearsed her answer many times.

"I help people make top-shelf decisions in work and life by always providing super premium products, service, thinking, and partnership."

"Brian, what do you think when she answers my question of 'What do you do?' with that response?"

Brian answered, "Well, I immediately think she's confident and smart. I know that she knows who she is. I would be intrigued to find out more about her."

Jack and Tracy both smiled.

"How long did it take you to get that answer the way you wanted it?"

"About two months. First I had to make a decision about what I wanted to be known for. Then I had to work on the purpose statement."

Brian interjected, "Purpose statement?"

Tracy continued, "Yes, when someone asks what you do, it's easy to give your job title. But it doesn't say anything about you as a person. If someone asks what do you do and you say, I'm in real estate. I'm a nurse. I'm in finance. I sell insurance. I'm an administrative assistant. Whatever you say immediately defines what you do for a living, but it doesn't allow you to brand yourself as different from the crowd."

Jack chimed in, "Brian, a purpose statement is something you create based on how you view your purpose in life. Not just in your job, but in all aspects of your life. Your personal brand is a shift in thinking. Your brand never shuts down. You are who you are and what you do 24/7. So, to have a job personality and a home personality are counterproductive to your overall personal brand and the energy it would take to maintain two different or competing brands. Volvo isn't safety during the day and speed at night. It's just one brand known specifically for one thing. You want a safe car, and there is only one choice. You can't be all things to everyone. A purpose statement takes what you want to be known for and helps you apply it to any situation that may come up in work or life. It helps you make better decisions. It starts with the phrase, 'I help people.'"

"I help people . . . ," Brian repeated.

"Yes. Tracy, say yours again," Jack stated.

"I help people make top-shelf decisions in work and life by always providing super premium products, service, thinking, and partnership."

"Brian, I'll ask you . . . does this work as a guiding principle if Tracy's friend asks her advice about a boyfriend or if a client asks her about which wines to stock?"

Brian thought for a few seconds. "Sure. But how did you come up with top shelf and super premium? What does that mean?"

Tracy stepped in, "That is usually the second or third question I get if people ask me what I do. It helps me then tell a story about what I do and why I describe myself in that way. If you look in the speed rack underneath where Jack is standing, you will see all of the house brand liquors. The cheaper stuff that you use to make drinks when people just ask for a vodka soda, gin and tonic, tequila sunrise. Those are called house brands. Generic and the cheapest."

"Yes, I broke one of those last night," Brian interjected.

"Not a big deal. It was the cheap stuff. Now, if you look on the back bar you will see about a hundred bottles of liquor. Those are the ones with the recognizable labels, the more popular brands. Some would be considered premium brands. Higher-quality and higher-priced than the house brands. The best of the best are considered super premium. Those are the highly regarded brands. Those are the best and usually the highest-priced because to certain customers, they have the most value. People are willing to pay more for those because of their quality and perceived value. Never break those! Those super premium brands are usually sitting on the top shelf, high above the house and premium brands.

"That's me. I'm super premium. I'm top shelf. I believe that certain customers will appreciate me for the unique value I bring to their lives and their businesses. So, that's how I describe what I do. The terminology is from the industry I'm in. It means 'the best there is,' and it's meaningful to me when I explain it."

Jack was smiling a big smile. "You used to hate it when people would ask what you did."

Tracy said, "Of course I did. Everyone hates that question. What do you do? Tell me about yourself. Any interview I ever went on started with that one. No one likes that question because most people have not taken the time to truly figure out who they are and what they stand for. You helped me do that."

"And now?"

"And now I make more than I ever have in my life and feel fulfilled both at work and home because I'm not only creating value for myself, but also for anyone I come in contact with. My priorities and my principles come out loud and clear through my purpose statement. That is my identity. Super Premium. It's even on my card."

Tracy looked more intently at Brian.

"I know it's a lot to take in. It was for me as well. But I took the time and figured it out. It's made all the difference in my life. Took me two months to get it exactly right. Now it's my brand, my personal marketing message, and my purpose."

Brian nodded. "Jack, do you have a purpose statement?"

"Of course. Mine is . . . I help people get happier."

"That doesn't tell me you are a bartender, though," Brian responded.

"Nope. It's not supposed to. That's not how I choose to define myself. It's supposed to tell you my purpose and what I stand for. If you want to know what I do for a living, that can be your second question, but I am not going to let you put me into a pile of people the first moment you meet me. As a bartender, bar owner, and as a person, for me there is no greater purpose than helping someone get happier. Granted, sometimes it will take a double scotch to help them get there, but sometimes it's just a listening ear or some friendly advice. When I come to work, my purpose is to help people get happier. And, if you think about it, what better place to accomplish that goal? No matter if you are sad or celebrating, my role is to get you to a better place . . . to make you happier."

"So, when I go on my next interview and the person says tell me about yourself, what do I say?" Brian asked.

Jack motioned for Tracy to take the answer.

"You say, I help people . . ."

"I help people what?" Brian asked.

"That's for you to figure out. It's a purpose statement and no two are the same. I actually love Kelly's purpose statement," Tracy responded.

"You know hers too?"

"You know what, that's the really cool thing about identifying yourself with a purpose rather than a title. You get the chance to tell a story about it. And it's always the story that people remember."

Jack interjected, "It's a great story."

"So, Kelly's brand is 'Punch,'" Tracy said.

"You mean like fruit punch?" Brian asked.

"Not exactly. Kelly's purpose statement is, I help people have more punch in their lives."

"Punch?"

"So, here's the story, and Jack, let me know if I get it wrong. Legend has it that Kelly was working one night, and the bar was packed. People were everywhere. All of a sudden, a guy she just served started banging on the bar trying to get her attention, but she had moved on to the next person. But he kept banging on the bar. When she turned to see what the fuss was, the guy and a few of his friends were waving their arms to get her attention. She stopped what she was doing and went over to see what the issue was.

"The guy said to her, 'Hey, sweetie, this drink has no punch.' Everyone was now staring at her, like 'what was she going to do? and the guy had a stupid look on his face, like 'how are you going to make this right?' He leaned in close and said again, 'This drink has no punch.'

"So, she balled up her fist and punched the guy as hard as she could and said, 'Did you feel that punch?!'

"The guy was so stunned he didn't know what to do and eventually just slinked away from the bar. His friends all moved forward and threw 50 bucks on the bar and said, 'That's for you. He's been a jerk all night. We love you. Let's do some shots!!'"

"She punched a customer?" Brian asked.

Jack nodded.

"Are you allowed to do that?"

"Not really. But he was obnoxious." Jack laughed.

"The point of the story," Tracy continued, "is those guys who threw Kelly the 50 dollar tip became loyal customers, and the guy complaining actually apologized at the end of the night for being a jerk and never complained again. They still, to this day, come in to see her and retell that story almost every time they're here."

"I wish I could have punched a few of my customers," Brian added.

"Me too," Tracy added. "I wouldn't recommend it. Not great for your brand. Unless you're Kelly. So, the takeaway is, when Jack asked Kelly about her purpose statement and what she wanted to be known for, she thought about the moment when she stood out, the story behind it, and what she really wanted to be known for as a bartender, an actress, and a person. And, if you know Kelly, she will literally or figuratively give some punch to your life when you need it, or even if you don't. Jack . . . how did I do?"

"Tracy, couldn't have told it better myself. Her personal brand can be summed up with that story and her word. Brian, would you agree?"

"Absolutely. I was always a little afraid of her to begin with so this proves I wasn't imagining things."

"Brian, that's a strong personal brand. Tracy's Super Premium is a strong personal brand. It wasn't always her brand. It was her aspirational brand that she had to work at every day until she became known for it. What you have to ask yourself is, *What do you want to be known for?* Once you figure out your identity and what you stand for, you welcome those 'What do you do' and 'Tell me about yourself' questions. Eventually, you don't even have to tell your story anymore because people are actually doing it for you."

Tracy pulled a few folders out from her bag and put them in front of Jack.

"You ready to talk about those super premium tequilas?"

"You bet."

Brian got up from the bar stool and shook hands with Tracy.

"Thank you for sharing," Brian said. "Makes me realize that all this time I've been nothing more than a title and a job function. Doing the work, but not really thinking beyond the day in front of me."

"You can change that," Tracy said. "I did. Here is the most important lesson I learned: if you don't take the time to figure out what your brand is, other people will do it for you. So, in effect, by not taking charge of managing your brand and your reputation, you are putting your future and your value into the hands of others. You, me, and everyone in the world has the opportunity to take charge of our lives and the perceived value we bring to others. The key is to take the time to really see yourself."

That night, Brian was on a mission. He was determined not to be thought of as the weak link. Jack was making people happier. Kelly was adding "punch" and passion to every interaction she had. What was his purpose? As he took care of each customer that night, he thought back to his time in sales. How did he help people? With all of the sales training and sales models and sales motivation, did anyone once ask him how he helped people? Sales scripts and role-plays never once addressed helping people. Find pain points and sell against the pain. Sort of helping, but more about selling. Closing techniques and external motivational contests never once talked about helping people. His products helped people. His team of experts helped people. Clients needed collaboration and direction. They needed someone to help them make better choices.

Yes, Brian thought. That would be a start. *I help people make the best decisions.* In the past, he thought the best choice was always the choice he was selling. But what if he really believed that his role was not to sell something but to help someone make the best choice to achieve their goals? Clients would see value in that. That would be a good purpose statement, or at least the start of one.

After another nonstop evening of serving house, premium, and super premium drinks, Brian made it home with even more money in his pocket than the night before. He only broke two glasses the entire night, and even Kelly, who showed up later in the evening, said he had improved beyond what she thought possible. She even punched him on the shoulder, which Jack said was kind of like a respectful hand-shake for her.

As he walked into his house at 5:00 a.m. and put his keys in the bowl on the counter, he felt his phone vibrate. He took it out of his pocket and opened the TIP e-mail from Jack.

TIP

LABELS

I recently had the opportunity to sit in on a focus group marketing session for a liquor company that was trying to assess whether customers would buy some of the new products they were considering putting out to the market.

I, along with some fellow bar owners, were hired for the day as a focus group to spend some time sitting in a room looking at bottles and packaging, tasting certain liquors, and giving our opinion of how we thought these development products would stand out in the real world, where shelf space is already limited. We were on the front line of this industry, and the company wanted to know our opinion. Some might even call us "thought leaders."

The products were inanimate objects, unable to answer back. They were unable to defend themselves, but I imagined what it would be like to have people sitting in a room telling you what they liked about you and hated about you. What would it be like to have someone criticize your shape, your color, your quality?

Most people would not fare too well listening to that kind of criticism, which is why most people do not solicit feedback from friends, co-workers, family, and bosses about themselves. People don't want to be criticized. But, the truth is, you are already being judged.

In marketing, most products go through some sort of focus group assessment. No company is going to invest the millions of dollars it is going to take to launch something new into the marketplace without some sort of measurable research.

What if we could have our own focus group in work and life? What if we could have a team of people we trust tell us the truth about how we are being perceived? What if we decided to relaunch our personal brand in a way that is more attractive to the customers who need the help we can give them?

The truth is, we can have that focus group anytime we want if we are willing to put ourselves out there and listen for the feedback. If we are willing to hear what people have to say about us—good or bad—we can get the feedback we need to make the necessary adjustments to be more successful in our work and our relationships. Self-awareness is not just about being introspective.

It's really very simple. Ask the experts—the people who know you best, who work with you, who care about you—what they think of your brand. Accept the answers. Adapt what is relevant to make you better. Pretty simple formula. You just have to be willing to ask, and then really listen.

Take It Personally,

Jack

11 The Bear

The alarm went off and Brian threw himself into the shower to wake up before racing to get to Drew's soccer game. There would be no extra sleep for the bear today. The park was only two miles from the house, and he got there just as the teams were taking the field, waving to Drew as his son assumed his position on defense.

He found Jen and the girls sitting on a blanket on the sideline and plopped himself down.

"Grrrrrrr!" growled Sara.

"Grrrrrr!" he growled back. Brian grabbed her and held her upside down over his head. She started to playfully scream. Kyra, sensing her sister needed some help, toddled over to them and started punching Brian, shouting, "Bad Bear!"

Brian put Sara down, gave Kyra a kiss on the head, and then leaned over to kiss Jen.

"A good night?" she asked.

"It was. Good money and learned a few things," he responded. "So, I have a question for you. It might seem weird, but answer honestly."

"Okay."

"What's my brand?"

"What do you mean? Like, what brands do you use?"

"No. I mean, if I am known for one thing and only one thing, the way Volvo is known for safety, what would it be? What word best describes my brand?"

Jen thought for a moment.

"Well, you are a good father. You are kind. Patient, most of the time. You are caring. You have a temper, though. Sometimes you can be a jerk. You leave the seat up a lot. One word? Really?"

"Yes, one word."

"That's hard."

Sara ran across the blanket full steam into Brian's back, knocking him forward. At four years old, she already had the shoulders of a distance swimmer.

"You are THE BEAR!" she shouted, standing over him as he lay motionless.

"Da bear," Kyra shouted as well as she stepped on his hand.

"We must tame The Bear," Sara said to her sister.

"Da Bear," repeated Kyra.

Brian covered up into a fetal position to protect himself as the girls continued to walk on him and pull at his hair.

"Actually," Jen said, "I think the girls are right."

"Right about what?"

"That is your brand. The Bear. Your brand is like a bear."

"How so?"

"Well, a bear is protective. Fierce. But also cuddly."

"It has to be one thing. I don't want to be cuddly."

"Maybe that's the problem. A bear is many things to many people."

He thought about the bottle, sitting there, taking the judgment. Don't defend and don't judge. Listen to the feedback. Let the focus group speak. He liked the word *fierce*. But he was not fierce, and that was the point. He was once fierce, but not anymore. This was supposed to be reinvention. This was supposed to be the creation of a new Brian, one that didn't just try. The new and improved Brian could be fierce. Powerful, strong, protective.

"Do you think I'm fierce?"

"That wouldn't be the word I would pick for you. Protective, maybe . . . but not fierce. You don't really like conflict. You can't even tell your mother we're not coming to Thanksgiving this year. Definitely not fierce. A passive-aggressive bear who doesn't want to hurt his mother's feelings. You're more of a peaceful bear. A kind bear."

"The kind bear must be tamed!" shouted Sara.

"Tame da bear," repeated Kyra.

"That's enough, you two," said Jen. "People are looking at us, and you are supposed to be watching your brother's game. Turn around, sit down, and eat the lunch I packed for you. Leave your father alone."

Sara turned to Brian and whispered, "I'll get you later, Kind Bear."

Funny, Brian thought, that his four-year-old daughter was more intimidating than he had ever been at work. He used to be intimidating. He was feared on the field in high school and college. What happened? The bear. The cuddly bear. It wasn't what he would like people to say about him, but it was honest feedback.

Brian thought about how different he was today from what he was like earlier in his life. At 19 he was a wild bear. He played three seasons of sports in high school, went to all the parties, was a college athlete, and had a great time.

That continued through his twenties and at 29 he was married. No kids yet, so he and Jen had a lot of fun together, traveling and learning about the world. Unafraid. His sales career was hitting a good period, but he still had a lot to learn. He was a curious bear. Today, he couldn't remember the last time he had read a book that wasn't assigned for work. If he had free time, he watched TV, mostly cartoons with the kids and sports by himself or with his friends. He always read the same sections of the paper, scanning what he found interesting, and only reading the articles that already validated his current interests.

He assumed most people were the same. We eventually just settle into the things we like or focus on the things that reinforce what we already believe. Who really wants to change? If things are good, and even if they're not, change is scary. At least you know what to expect in the world you currently work and live in. Most people change only when they have to, when they are forced to. The vast majority of people don't go looking for change. They don't challenge themselves on a daily basis to learn new things and create new experiences. They are too busy trying to protect what already exists, even if it's just average. The curious bear dies and fearful bear takes over.

At 39, he felt like a circus bear. Dance. Do the job, make people happy, get three square meals a day, but don't question the ringmaster. Don't step outside the circle, circus bear, or you lose it all. Wild circus bears usually get put down. That was the thinking that got him where he was today. He needed to be more fearless.

He thought about what life might be like if he continued to dance. What kind of bear would he be at 49? What would be "premium" in 10 years? It would have to be different. It would have to be more. It would have to be better. But only he could make that happen. He had to be responsible for his own future and accountable for whatever results came from his action or inaction, positive or negative.

Brian overheard a conversation in the bar between two people who were obviously trying to motivate one another. One said to the other, "The only difference between you today and you a year from now are the new things you read, the new people you meet, and the new experiences you have." Brian wrote that phrase down.

This whole bartending experience, even after a week, was forcing him to meet and talk to new people he might never otherwise even look at, let alone have a discussion with. The bar provided him a chance to interact with the personalities of many different people from all walks of life. They weren't long conversations. Sometimes, the interaction was only a few minutes, but he was learning and growing just by listening to new people talk about new things. Some wanted to talk.

Some wanted to know his story. But even the shortest conversations connected him with strangers, and were giving him a sense of confidence that he remembered existed before all of the rejection he faced after close to 17 years as a sales guy. Fear of loss killed the wild bear and the curious bear. We lose our ability to be curious when the fear of the unknown is stronger than our willingness to take even the smallest risk.

What kind of bear did he want to be? Fierce. Fearless. Focused. Ferocious. Yes. Definitely one of those.

12 Position Yourself

Whenever the clock struck 2:00 a.m., if he was awake, it always gave Brian a little chuckle. His dad, when trying to impose curfews and get him and his siblings to make better decisions in their own lives, would always say, "If you're out past 2:00 a.m., you're only looking for trouble." His dad was an undercover cop, so there was a lot of experience coming from that statement. As a bartender, Brian agreed, there was also a lot of truth.

Yet, the Saturday night of week two at Crossroads, something good happened after 2:00 a.m.

"Can I get a glass of water?" the man asked.

"Sure," Brian said without looking up.

When he poured the water, he looked up to hand it to the customer. He recognized the man. He wasn't sure where from, though.

"I know you, right?" Brian asked.

"Coach!" Jack screamed from the other end of the bar.

And then it dawned on Brian who this gray-haired man was. Coach Hal Babson was a Hall of Fame college football coach.

"Coach, great to see you. Thanks for coming in," Jack said.

"Anytime, Jack. We had some big alumni dinner downtown that let out about a half hour ago. Otherwise, I would have been in sooner. All those 'glory days' stories can go on sometimes a bit too long, but it's always great catching up with my former players."

"You met Brian?" Jack asked.

"Yes, just now."

"Coach, it's okay if I call you Coach, right? Big fan." Brian shook his hand.

"Yes, call me Coach. Everyone else does. Even my wife."

"Really?" Brian said.

"No, not really. Just kidding with you, Brian. She calls me Hal. Coach is my brand. And when I leave the room people say I'm mean and tough, but fair."

"Personal brand?"

"Yeah, yeah . . . I don't call it personal brand," Coach said to Brian. "That's Jack and his fancy brand strategy talk. I call it your reputation. I call it 'your shadow,' and I used to tell my players that your reputation will follow you wherever you go. It follows you and every single person you hang out with. So, we didn't call it branding. We called it, do the right thing and surround yourself with the right people, or I'll kick you in the ass and then I'll kick you off my team."

Brian thought that between Kelly punching people and Coach kicking them in the ass, this whole idea of personal branding could be considered a contact sport.

"I played for Coach Babson," Jack said. "He was the one who taught me all about having a strong sense of self. So, since I knew he was going to be in the neighborhood, I asked him to come in and talk to you about your identity."

"Jack tells me you are between jobs," Coach said.

"Yes."

"So, you're looking for a new team?"

"Well, yeah, I'm looking for a new company."

"No, you're looking for a new team. The company is not going to hire you. A person with needs who is in charge of a team within that company is going to hire you to be part of that team. Once you look at it that way, you will have a much easier time of finding a new position. That leader of that team has a vision. His or her team has necessary positions to deliver on that vision. You with me?"

"Yes, I understand. I also played ball and had a tough but fair but not as good a coach as you, so I get it," Brian added.

"You played in college?"

"Yes."

"Great. So, here's something you may not know but might have experienced. Kids who either graduate out of their sport or get hurt during their college careers and can't play anymore are up to 20% more likely to suffer severe depression when they stop playing their sport. Any idea why?"

"Obviously, they miss what they have been doing their whole lives. It happened to me. I played from the time I was eight years old through college, till my junior year," Brian stated.

"What happened junior year?"

"I got hurt. Spine and shoulder injury. A bit of nerve damage. Couldn't play my senior year. Had to medically retire. I was devastated. I guess you could say I felt incomplete."

"Depressed?"

"Yes."

"Questioned who you were?"

"Every day."

"Lost your identity?"

"Yes. I was no longer an athlete."

"And your whole life from that day up until this point you have been searching for a team, any kind of team to make you feel whole again?"

"Pretty much."

"And you thought your past company was that team."

"Not the way I felt about my sports teams, but yes. I felt like I was a part of something bigger than myself. I wore the branded golf shirts and had the swag bags with the corporate logo on them, and, yeah, I guess you could say I felt as much of a part of a team as I could."

"Brian, your company is not your team. Your company is like the school you graduated from. That's the bigger brand. When you go in for an interview, that college you graduated from will be a brand that either means something or it doesn't to the person hiring you. They may be impressed or they may not."

"I like to think I went to a good school."

"That's great, but at the end of the day, the better school brand doesn't matter if you can't help someone deliver the vision. The person hiring you wants someone who fills a position on his team with the best talent available, who stands for the same things he or she stands for. They care about the school brand but only as part of the decision process. That label will help them get to the final two or three choices for the position."

"I understand," Brian responded.

Kelly came running down to where Brian was standing and practically shoved him out of the way. She reached across the bar to give Coach a peck on the cheek.

"Coach! Great to see you."

"You too, Kell Bell. Punch anybody out tonight?"

"Not tonight, but there's still time on the clock."

Kelly ran back to the point where two new customers had just stepped up to the bar. Coach turned back towards Brian.

"That girl has always scared me a little bit," Coach said.

"So, you were saying the company and the school are the bigger brand."

"Right. And, within each school there are teams. Sports teams, clubs, academic teams, music teams, debate teams. You name it. You could find a few hundred teams at each school, just like you could find a few hundred teams at each big company. You won't play for every team. So, you need to decide what team you want to be on and make that team the best it can be.

"When I was the coach for the football team, I didn't care as much about what the rest of the teams were doing. If the other teams were doing well, that was good for the school, but not necessarily for my team. I didn't care about the basketball team or the lacrosse team. I cared about my team. My team had a brand. We had a very strong brand because I picked the best people for each position. Not just the best athletes—the best people. If you didn't fit with my culture, I didn't care how talented you were. You had to fit all aspects of my team to be chosen by me."

"So, you're saying I need to focus on helping the hiring manager and his or her team. If I do that, then I also help the company by making the team brand stronger. And based on my conversations over the past week or so, I need to be known for one thing that is essential to the team."

"Bingo. Your reputation is essential, but you can't be everything to everyone. I've seen people try to be everything, but no one is good at everything. You are better off if you have a strength or an expertise that is essential to the team, that gets results no one can match."

"What do you mean?"

"I'll explain in terms of when I used to do recruiting. When I looked for someone to join my team whether they were an athlete, an assistant coach, the team manager, or the water boy, I focused on their one greatest talent to get the results I needed for that position. Everyone has specific skills that are unique. I'm sure you have certain talents that no one else has. Right now you might be questioning your uniqueness, but find those talents; find what you are best at that can help a leader fill an essential position. Know what powers you have that make you an expert, and then you will have the confidence to put yourself out there for the right team. Know your greatest strength and highlight it. The right team will find you. Position yourself in a way that highlights the one thing that only you can bring to the role and the one thing that team needs most. It's easy to get the job when you are the only candidate for that unique position."

Brian realized that Coach was saying the same things Jack was saying, but it terms he could completely relate to. He was trying to get onto any team, taking any position that would have him. Instead, he should be looking for a team that needed him and the unique skills that only he had to offer.

"Brian, it's not complicated. As a coach, I just called it simply finding the best talent possible at the position I needed, who wouldn't need a kick in the ass. And, if I found a kid who had a great attitude with the best skills for the position, I'd do whatever I needed to get that kid on my team. In business, if you are the CEO, you pick great leaders who hire other great leaders who then hire other great employees. No matter who you are, if you are in charge of hiring someone, you want someone with a specific skill to make your team better. Brian, your job is to know your one true strength and find a way to make sure everyone else knows it as well."

Brian nodded.

"My boy, you will find another team. But you have to be valuable to the person recruiting you. Forget the logo and the benefits of the corporate brand. There are too many people who do that. I went to this school. I work for this company. Who cares?! One day your weak reputation that is hiding behind the stronger reputation of the company brand is going to be found out. Obviously, you wouldn't be between jobs if you were the right guy in the right position on the right team. Make your strength so powerful that the right team would be honored to have you. Remember, no one will hire you if you don't have the skills to make their team better."

Brian nodded.

"Jack! I'm leaving," Coach called out.

He turned to Brian.

"Good luck, Brian. You can do this."

They shook hands, and Coach walked out the door with a wave to Kelly.

Brian realized that if he did not make a single dollar that evening, it wouldn't matter.

After Coach left the bar that night, business picked up again slightly till about 3:30 a.m. Rather than leave early like Jack said he could, Brian stayed to help clean up and count tips. Brian never stayed late at his previous job. At least not in the past three or four years. Going beyond the norm was a personal brand that did not exist for him in the past.

He finally got home, but he couldn't go to sleep. So many things he wanted to do differently. He had wasted so much time being average. Coach was right. After he got hurt in college, he was not the same. He still wanted success, but something died in him. He became human. He had powers, but they were no longer superpowers. He felt invincible in college. Then the real world and work and his family became his priorities. So, forget being close to invincible. He just tried to get by or get around whatever obstacles occurred. You just lose a bit of yourself each day, he thought, until you don't even really know who you are anymore.

No! That would not be him anymore. He could change. He would change.

13 Communicate Your Brand

"Jack's going to be late," Kelly called down the bar.

It was Friday of week number three, and Brian was starting to get familiar with the routines of Crossroads. He nodded to Kelly as he continued to cut the lemons and limes for the drink garnish trays.

He had never worked with Kelly alone. She was usually out on an audition or a rehearsal or shooting an episode of something and was always the last one in to work. This Friday she didn't have anything going, and Jack needed to come in late.

He only broke one glass the previous Saturday and in only four shifts was beginning to pick up his pace enough to increase his tip contribution to "average." Definitely a step up from being labeled "the monkey."

"You're doing better," Kelly approached him.

"Well, it is just cutting lemons and limes. I think I should be able to handle fruit without an issue," Brian responded.

She smiled.

"No. I mean the work. Taking care of the customers. You care about getting better. And, it's showing. So, just wanted to say that."

Brian felt a sense of pride. He couldn't remember the last time anyone said something like that to him. Never underestimate the power of recognition.

"Thanks," he said. "I'll never be as fast as you, but you and Jack are good teachers."

"No. No you won't, and hopefully you'll be out of here before you get really good at it. I've been bartending for a while now, as a means to an end, because it gives me the freedom to be the actress I want to be, and audition for the roles I find meaningful and important."

Brian continued to cut the fruit.

"What's it like? Auditioning and that sort of thing. I mean, I was a sales guy so I understand the whole rejection thing, but it has to be frustrating to keep putting yourself out there."

Kelly thought for a moment and then gave an answer that sounded like she had been preparing her whole life.

"It's when you stop putting yourself out there, and stop taking chances and stop feeling like the next time will be the moment your life is going to change . . . that's worse than any rejection anyone could ever face. When you know who you are, and know there is a role out there that you're born to fill, that's all the motivation you should need."

He never thought of it like that. Everyone has a role. They don't have to be actors or actresses, but everyone at his company had a role that they were born, or at least trained, to play.

The finance people were good with numbers. The operations people were good with processes and analytics. And the salespeople were good at making connections and solving problems for prospects and clients. That was his role, until it wasn't.

"Have you ever been fired from an acting job?" Brian asked.

Kelly thought for a moment.

"No. Not fired, but by not being hired for a role when I audition, I always feel like I am being fired. Because in my mind, when I walked in the door, I felt like the role was mine. Not always. Not when I was young. But, when I started to think of my personal brand and how I needed to communicate what makes me unique to a complete stranger who doesn't know me, that's when my perspective changed. So, I guess you could say I've been 'fired' a hell of a lot more times than you."

"And you keep coming back for more."

"I do. Because I know my purpose is to help tell stories. I know that I have a range of skills and strengths that include a well-developed imagination, emotional intelligence, and the ability to be physically expressive. Acting is really the only thing I've ever wanted to do and the thing that I'm best at in my life. There is no alternative plan for me. The bartending allows me to pursue my ultimate goal. So, to me, any audition I go on is a chance for me to further educate someone about who I am and the uniqueness I can bring to the role."

Role. Not just an acting term.

"So, let me ask you," Brian turned to Kelly. "How do you convince someone you've just met that you are the perfect person for the role you want?"

Kelly smiled.

"An interview is an audition. Yes?"

"Yes." Brian nodded.

"Okay. So, here's what happens in an audition. I get the call from my agent to go to a casting director's office. I sit in a waiting room along with anywhere from 10 to 30 women who look very similar to me, because the role calls for a certain kind of look. I sit with my headshot and résumé and wait my turn until I get called into a room where I get the chance to show why I should be chosen over the hundreds of women who have been called in to audition for the role. If I do it right, or if I am worth another look, I get a callback and then go in and audition for the director of the show, film, or commercial. If necessary, there could be another callback, at which time I know my chances of getting the role are better."

Brian realized that an audition for an acting role was no different from an interview for a job. Basically, you send in your résumé or have an "agent" or headhunter do it for you. If you have the right skills and character to be considered, you get a meeting, but you're initially part of a giant pile of résumés from people who could fill the role as well as you, at least on paper. If you do well on the interview, you get a chance to meet more people and see if you are a good fit for the role and the company.

"How long is the audition?" Brian asked.

"Depends. Could be two minutes. Could be five or ten on a callback."

"That's it?"

"That's it."

"That's crazy. How do you convince someone to hire you in five minutes?"

"Brian, I've been trying to figure that out for years, but here's the deal; you really only have about seven seconds to make an impression, and then it's all about living truthfully under imaginary circumstances. That is the definition of acting. Being truthful under imaginary circumstances. You know bad acting when you see it, right?"

"Sure. It's like the actor is there physically but not invested emotionally."

Kelly punched Brian on the arm.

"There you go! That's exactly it. My audition and your next big interview have one thing in common: we both need to be able to convince our future employers that we can do the job before we actually have the job. We need to somehow get them to imagine what life would be like with us in the role that they need to fill. For you, they need to imagine how your co-workers, customers, and anyone else that has contact with you is going to react to you being in that role. You have to make an emotional connection, and to do that you have to communicate your truthful and authentic self in a way that removes any doubt that you can fill the role better than anyone else."

Brian realized that his whole career was an audition. In sales, he had one job, to convince his prospects that he and his company could do the job, before actually doing the job. He needed to use all of his skills to tap into the imagination and emotion of the prospect and let that person's brain do the majority of the work. Imagination. Will this person be right for the role I need to fill?

There is always a leap of faith when someone makes a new hire. They have to rely on instinct as well as the data in front of them. But, in all cases, it comes back to the imagination and visualization of the person doing the hiring. Can they see a positive future for the team with this person in a specific role? In a way, every team leader who has the chance to hire someone is playing director and casting a role for his or her team.

"So, how do you do it? How do you get the person casting or hiring to take a leap of faith on someone they've never worked with before?" Brian asked.

"Brand."

"Brand?"

"Yes. How you communicate your brand is going to have a huge effect on whether someone hires you or not."

"Well, brand is all we talk about in this place, so I'm not surprised."

"My brand is . . . ?"

"Punch."

"Great. You heard the story. Well, most casting directors in town know that story as well . . . because I tell it. I'm not looking for the role of the fairy princess. Unless it's a modern take on the fairy princess as a badass princess from the wrong side of town. Or a fairy princess that just got out of the military. Or a fairy princess that becomes a cop because the king and all her prince brothers are cops. You get the picture. I know who I am. And, every chance I get, I communicate my brand and my character. I bring 'punch' to everything I do.

I don't try to be all things to all people. My agent knows the roles that are right for me, which means I never even see opportunities that I know are a waste of my time. So, when I walk into a room, no matter what the role is, I am confident the role I'm auditioning for matches my brand. And I know the interpretation of that role is what will set me apart from my competitors."

"I'm still not sure what my perfect role is," Brian interjected.

"Then you don't know who you are yet, or the value you bring. And that's okay. But, until you know who you are and what makes you better than anyone else, you are going to walk into an interview grasping for words and ideas that are not authentically your own. You need to bring *you* to the role you want. You need to come with ideas and opinions of how the role will be better or more dynamic with you instead of some-one else. Until you know who you are, you can't walk in the room with any extra value. You'll just be labeled a stand-in."

"Stand-in?"

"My agent, when she first took me on, said something I will never forget. She said this world has two types of people. Stand-ins and stand-outs. Stand-ins are a dime a dozen. They are substitutes for the real thing. A stand-in does just that; they stand in the hot lights, or stand in the cold weather and hold a spot for the crew to set up for technical purposes, so when it's time for the star to do his or her thing, they aren't wasting precious time. The stand-in is helpful, makes union wages, and is easily replaceable. They are just holding space. The stand-out is the star. They are the ones you can't take your eyes off of. They are engaging and make you want to either be them, or be with them. You are either a stand-in or stand-out. So, unless you know who you are and the extra value you can bring to a role to better execute the bigger story, you aren't going to have the confidence to walk into a room and demand the role."

Demand the role. *Demand.* Such a powerful word. When was the last time he had the confidence to demand anything? When was the last time he questioned the status quo or had a thought about how to make his role or his company better? Auditioning is not just for people without jobs, he thought. Every day is an audition, no matter what job you have. You have to come to work like it's day one and create something that no one has ever seen before. You have to have a point of view and say and do things that are not just whatever you think the manager wants to hear. You have to come with ideas and opinions and interpretations on how to make things run better, faster, smarter, and stronger.

To be a stand-out in the role you already have, you have to audition for your job every day. Because, if you're not putting the best version of yourself out there to your boss and your team and your customers, you can be sure someone else is. And your role is quickly going to be someone else's role. If you're not making someone else's job easier, mainly your boss's, then you're making it harder. There is no in-between.

Brian thought how his brand probably reflected on his manager's brand at his previous job. Actually, his manager famously used to say, "If I have to do your job for you, what do I need you for?" So, if his manager wanted to be seen as a leader of exceptional employees, what did the guy who was just making quota look like? Probably a blemish on the team and his manager's reputation.

"So, let's say I figure out who I am and the role I was born to have. How do I walk into a room and demand a role?" Brian asked.

"You have to bring it."

"Bring it?"

"Yeah. Bring it!"

Kelly jumped up onto the bar and was now standing where people would be soon eating their food. Very dramatic move.

Looking down at him she said, "You have one opportunity to make an impression on someone. Jack told you, and I said it too. You have seven seconds before someone makes a judgment about you. And within 60 seconds, about 90% of someone's perception of you is complete. Done. Within a minute, someone has decided if they want to work with you, or not. That means the moment you say hello, you better bring it!"

"Yeah, I get it. But bring what?"

"Your best self. Your presence of confidence and authority."

Kelly jumped down from the bar.

"You are judged by your presence. Do you have personal presence, Brian?"

"I'd like to think I do."

"Nope. Horrible answer. I'd like to think I do? How about Yes! You know what I thought when I first met you?"

"I'm afraid to ask."

"I thought, hey, here is a nice guy. Nice, but not very confident. Shoulders rolled forward, looks down a lot. Weak handshake. Doesn't seem very passionate. Voice tends to trail off. You didn't even need to tell me you were fired. I could have told you that if you weren't fired it would only be a matter of time."

Brian shook his head and smiled a half smile. She was tough.

"Come on," she said, "I'm not telling you anything you don't already know. If I asked you what you did before you got fired, you would have told me you were a Justa."

"Justa?"

"Yes. I hear it all the time. Justa. Just a sales guy. Just a bartender. Just a meeting planner. Just a broker. Just a teacher. Just a whatever. What do you do? I'm Justa. Nice to meet you, Justa. Now get out of my face because you are draining the energy from this entire room. Anyone who starts with the phrase 'I'm Justa' to describe themselves deserves to be fired."

She was on a roll, and Brian was actually enjoying the performance. It seemed that Kelly had somehow transitioned into one of the characters she would be auditioning for. Tough teacher at a school where every student needs some tough love and definitely no time for anyone's self-pity. She could probably use this as a monologue for one of her next big auditions. He would suggest it, but she'd probably hit him with a bottle.

"Do I get nervous for auditions? Of course I do. Especially when I get really close to landing the role. But if I walk in nervous and communicate anything other than what my brand is supposed to represent, then I've already lost. So I think about everything that makes up my personal presence."

"And what's that?"

"It's everything. We are all graded on how we say hello, if we smile, how we shake hands, the amount of eye contact we make, whether we have good posture, and even the kind of gestures we make with our hands. We win or lose a role based on the kind of energy we bring into the room with us. If we are engaging, confident, likable, passionate, and even humorous, we stand a much greater chance of winning the job than if we walk in like a Justa!"

Don't be a Justa. Got it, Brian thought. He really believed she might take a swing at him just for fun.

"Brian, it's really very simple. *Does your brand communicate a problem or a promise?* Within the first 60 seconds of meeting someone they are determining if you are going to help them or hurt them. And the really cool part is, you have the power and the skills to communicate your brand on your terms. You have the power to show people whether you are going to make their lives easier or harder. Isn't that empowering?"

Brian nodded. It was empowering, if not intimidating. He wasn't stupid. He knew that how he dressed and whether he made eye contact was important, but did he do it consistently? No. He didn't give it much thought at all. Even worse, he probably let his defeatist attitude get in the way of his opportunities.

"You had me at hello," Kelly blurted.

"*Jerry Maguire!*" Brian called out.

"Yes. When Tom Cruise goes into this whole explanation about how he wasn't complete without Renee Zellweger. He does this great monologue, and at the end she just says, 'You had me at hello.'"

"Classic scene."

"Yes, but that phrase is all about how you should make someone feel during an interview or audition. You should have them at your hello. And then anything afterwards is all about details and the promise of the value you bring. When you walk in the room and open your mouth, it should be . . . 'Done. That's a wrap. Give the guy the part.' You see what I'm saying?"

"I do."

"You have to think about the impression you make from the first moment someone interacts with your brand, even if you're not in the room. People are judged by how those impressions stick in the minds of the audience you are trying to influence. Remember that each time you interact with someone, it's another chance to make a positive impression and strengthen your brand. And when you communicate authentically based on knowing who you are and what you stand for, you will consistently convey confidence and credibility even when you're not around, which is what a great brand does. It makes people feel safe and secure. And when you do that, you can not only get whatever role you want, you can name your price."

Brian pointed to his watch.

"Not that I'm not loving the lesson, but it's time to open doors and get to work," he said.

Kelly pointed at her own watch and then back at Brian.

"Exactly," she said. "Time. And the next time I see you, leave Justa at home. Be authentic. Be passionate. Be bold."

She grabbed him by the shoulders.

"Be you. Be true."

14 What's Your Story?

Saturday morning Brian woke up and immediately went up to the attic of the house. He found the large plastic container marked BRIAN'S STUFF and carried it down to the living room. Inside he found all of the items from his past.

When his parents sold his childhood home to move to a warmer climate, they purged everything. There was no need to save anything, they said. The two-bedroom condo would only hold so much, and there was no way his dad was going to pay for a storage unit. So they gave Brian all of his saved childhood memories, just as they gave his siblings their memories and keepsakes. It was all there, packed up in one big giant container.

He rummaged through all of the pictures and short stories. He found the poem about "The Chickafant" he wrote when he was six years old, which his mother got published in a local kids' magazine. Part chicken. Part elephant. It was hideous. She bought 20 copies. There were yearbooks and trophies and pictures from birth all the way up to his wedding.

But he was looking for the one particular folder that might shed some light on what "be true" really meant.

There, under his high school graduation picture was the folder marked COLLEGE ESSAY. His mother saved everything.

He opened it up and saw the handwritten draft of the essay he wrote to get into college. At 18 years old, there is no regret. Sure, maybe you dated the wrong people, or you should have taken someone else to the prom, but those are the biggest issues for most teens. For the last three weeks, as his new colleagues and customers at Crossroads kept talking to him about his brand, and making a transition to a new life, he couldn't help but see the parallels of that time in his life when he was transitioning from high school to college.

As a senior in high school, you are forced to promote yourself. You are forced to sit at the kitchen counter and painfully think about all the things that make you awesome. How you help the community. Volunteer work. Examples of leadership. At 18 years old you must make a series of defining statements that are going to affect the rest of your life and then convey it with a unique voice that stands out from the crowd.

Brian remembered his guidance counselor telling him that the words he chose to describe himself would be how the admissions people would inevitably judge him. She didn't call it brand communication, but that's exactly what she meant. "Make a bold statement about your future and the success you are going to achieve and dare the world to prove you wrong."

As he read the essay, he could remember writing the words. They were the words of a student-athlete with lots of friends and a vision of the future that was crystal clear. His 18-year-old self was full of confidence and optimism. It was a good essay because he was sharing his truth about what made him unique and deserving to attend the college of his choice. He shared his skills and the value he would bring to the school both on the field and in the classroom. He even talked about actually being an ambassador for the school, long after he graduated. He was talking about brand alignment long before he knew what brand alignment even was.

Funny how that was the last time he could remember being such a self-promoter. He was always taught to be humble. If you do good work, you don't need to self-promote. You don't need to brag. Your reputation will speak for itself. The powerful people will eventually find you if you keep doing a good job. Unfortunately, it wasn't true, and he found out too late that who you know can be more important than what you know.

He wasn't always a Justa. But he hated office politics. So, when the good accounts started passing him by because the other salespeople were better office politicians, he fell back into a shell and started to cover up, hoping he could at least keep the work and the clients he had going. Little by little, things changed, and clients left. And, without a pipeline and a good territory, it was only a matter of time before quota was the best he could do.

How do you promote yourself without looking like a total suck-up?

The answer was right there in his own handwriting. Tell a great story about one experience that defines you. Don't brag. Educate. Educate them about the value you will bring to their world, just as you have done in your past. Like a college application, educate them with your numbers, your technical expertise, but most importantly, your "why." Perfect SAT scores are great, but they don't tell the whole story of your brand. Neither do your technical skills that can be replicated by 20 other people waiting in line for your job. Educate those with the power to choose you by sharing who you are and what you stand for. If you do it right, they will easily pick you over your fellow applicants because you have more to offer.

Help them make the choice easier. He read the essay over again. It was pretty good, but, man, how he hated writing it. How many fights did he get into with his parents, telling them the essay, the story, didn't matter. The numbers were good enough. But he was wrong. They were right. The admissions officer in charge of his application actually wrote him to say that his essay was the thing that pushed the committee to say yes. The grades were good. The sports helped. But the essay . . . the story . . . the truth . . . about who he was made the difference.

Brian put the essay back in the container and walked into the kitchen. He grabbed a notepad and a pen, and for the second time in his life sat down at a kitchen counter to write all of the reasons why someone should choose him. "Be true. Be you." That was the thought running through his mind, and at the top of the page he scribbled:

My Signature Story

15 Actions Build the Brand

O ver the next two weeks, Brian would meet many different people from all walks of life. Crossroads was where they came "to get happier" and share their own stories. He was learning more about human behavior and communication than he ever had in school or in his previous job.

Five weeks on the job at Crossroads, and finally his technical skills were acceptable. He might never be as fast as Jack or Kelly, but he felt good being able to take care of the middle of the bar. However, all the technical skills to date couldn't prepare him for the marathon.

Crossroads sits right at the 19-mile mark of the annual city marathon. They close off the street for the runners, but the businesses remain open. Crossroads, he found out, was where many spectators came to watch their friends run by, and then go into the bar and celebrate the fact that they, personally, were not running the marathon. 26.2 miles. Who the heck would want to do that?

Jack had asked Brian to do a double shift, so he worked Friday night, went home, slept for 4 hours, took a shower, and then returned to the bar for his own marathon: 14 straight hours of bartending. He was promised more money than he would make in two weeks of normal shifts, so how could he say no? Besides, the headhunters and job sites were slow getting him the kinds of interviews he was hoping for.

It had been two months since he was fired and he was starting to get antsy. The severance package was still covering the expenses, but he only had one more week of that. He had banked the five weeks cash from the bar so far, but if that ran out, they'd have to start dipping into savings.

He was working on his word. *Experience.* He heard Jack talk about it all the time. The best create an experience for their customers. In the past, at his old job, he had gotten to a point where he was so focused on selling, he didn't really think about creating an experience, other than closing the deal. *Service.* A good word, but not enough. *Create an experience.* Give all of yourself to a customer, project, or even a family member, and you will get everything in return that you deserve. TIP. Take the quality of the experience you create for another person, personally. Give more. Get more. If you do that, no matter what job you have, you win. That, he discovered, was his aspirational brand. As a sales person, he helped people make better choices, but his brand would be focused on *experience.* Jack had said his word should shoot him out of bed in the morning and make him rest soundly at night, only if he had fulfilled the promise of his brand to the most important people in his life.

Every day he walked into Crossroads, he actually cared about what he was doing. Sure, it was a bit mindless in comparison to the long sales cycle of selling to one of his former customers. But, for some reason, he truly cared about creating an experience for the people who wanted to come to Crossroads to "get happier."

By noon, the bar was open and starting to slowly fill up. On TV, the professional runners were already at the finish line drinking their sport drinks and taking pictures for the news stations. Around noon, the regular people who were running for personal victories were finally making their way up the avenue. It was a madhouse outside, with people screaming and cheering. They were holding signs of encouragement for family and friends. Just 7 more miles to go after running 19 might not sound like much, but Jack said the 19-mile mark is where they need the most encouragement to keep going.

Throughout the day a few of those runners even ran through the open doors at Crossroads to hug the couple sitting at the front of the bar.

The couple was Tom and Tara Traynor. They were as cute as their names sounded. They would come in on Friday nights after work and usually hang out with a large group of people dressed for the office but mentally ready for the weekend. It actually made Brian jealous from time to time, remembering his own group of colleagues that went out after work. He had never had the chance to interact with the Traynors, since their group was so large they would usually occupy a table in the back.

However, when yet another runner came into the bar to hug and take a picture with the couple, Brian had to ask what the deal was.

Tom laughed. "I'm a personal trainer, and I have a bunch of clients I work with who are running in the marathon today. I told them that I would set up camp here at the 19-mile mark.

I told them that if they needed the encouragement to keep going, I would be here. Most of them just want to finish, so I give them a hug, whisper something personal that I know will fire them up, and hope they have enough gas for the last 7 miles."

Tara jumped in. "And that group I'm always here with on Friday nights is my talent and performance development team from my organization. I'm the head of the department and a few of my co-workers are also running today. It started out as one woman trying to lose 30 pounds, and then evolved into an interdepartmental competition."

"So, you're both trainers," Brian stated. "And your name is Traynor."

"Yup. Talk about fulfilling your brand promise, right?" Tom said.

"That's cool," Brian said.

"I wasn't always a Traynor," Tara said, "but I've always been a trainer. I help people enhance skills and performance by changing, challenging, and championing beliefs and behaviors."

"I train the body. She trains the mind," Tom said.

At that moment, Jack made his way to the front of the bar and overheard the conversation.

"And, you were always a Traynor, but not always a trainer. Isn't that right, Tom?"

Tom smiled. "Yes, Jack. So, shall we tell the story yet again?"

"Yes, we shall. For the benefit of my friend, Brian, who is in the middle of restarting his career. There is no one better to tell him how to reinvent himself than you."

"You want to start it off?" Tom asked.

"Sure." Jack turned to Brian. "So, I'm playing softball in a bar league a few years back. I'm on third base and there's a fly ball to left field. I think it's deep enough, so I tag up and head for home. It's going to be close, so I slide head first. Well, as I slide, the catcher applies the tag to the back of my head. My face smacks the corner of home plate and splits my chin open."

Jack points to the bottom of his chin.

"My face is now covered in blood and won't stop bleeding, so someone gives me a towel, and I apply pressure and somehow they get me to the hospital emergency room, where I have to wait in the waiting room until I'm put in an exam room. After about half an hour, a resident doctor comes to take a look at me. Guess who the doctor is?"

Brian shrugs.

Jack points to Tom.

"So, this resident is telling me it will be about five hours before the plastic surgeon can come and stitch me up. The young doctor says he is really good at what he does and even though he is a resident, with the location of the cut on my chin, he could do the job just as well. He has an aura of confidence that makes me comfortable. Also, I don't feel like waiting five hours. I have to get to work, so I tell him to stitch it up."

Jack leans in further to show Brian the barely noticeable scar.

"I tell this young resident that if he gets the chance one day, he should come into my bar so I can properly thank him for helping me. Well, about three weeks later, Tom shows up to admire his handiwork and get a few free drinks, but proceeds to tell me that he's no longer a doctor. He's bailed on his residency because what he really wants to be is a personal trainer."

"You just told him the whole story. Why did you tell me to tell the story when you just told the whole story?" Tom playfully snapped.

Jack laughed. "Because I still can't believe that I let you stitch my face up, and three weeks later you quit. I'm lucky I don't look like one of those plastic surgeries gone wrong."

"I was a good doctor. Well trained. You had nothing to worry about."

Brian interjected, "So, you were a doctor and gave it up to be a personal trainer. Isn't that kind of backwards?"

"Yeah, but I hated it. I hated being a doctor. I was good at it. I'd make a good living if I took it all the way. But I knew it wasn't my purpose. I didn't want to cut people open or sew them back together. I have a lot of great friends who are phenomenal doctors in all areas of the profession. That's their purpose. But I wanted to do something different. I wanted to influence people to see themselves in the best possible light. My purpose is to help people become the best versions of themselves. My word . . . my brand . . . is *Transformation.*"

Jack left to take care of customers at the other end of the bar.

"So, you had to start over," Brian said to Tom.

"Yes. I started over. And, not everyone was supportive of my change."

Tom smiled at Tara.

"She thought she was getting a doctor. So did her parents, my parents, and all my parents' friends. But it just wasn't who I wanted to be. I stuck with it and thought I would grow to love it. Or maybe I stuck with it because everyone else wanted it for me. Not sure. When I made the decision to focus on helping people become the best version of themselves, something changed in me. I had balance. I had energy. I woke up every morning like I was on a mission. I couldn't wait to see what the day would bring or who it would bring into my world. I was curious. I wanted to continue to learn and grow so I could help others learn and grow."

Tara put her arm around her husband and gave him a kiss on the cheek.

"Are you married, Brian?" she asked.

"Yes. And three kids," he responded.

She nodded.

"I bet when you find your purpose, you will be a much better husband. I'm not saying you're not a good man or a good husband. But when someone is committed to themselves in a way that is fulfilling, it can be life changing for everyone around them. You can't commit to someone else if you're not committed to yourself first. That was definitely the case with Tom. Basically, he was an ass, until he wasn't."

Tom laughed. "I was. A big ass. I almost lost you."

"But then he had the guts to tell me and his parents and everyone else what he really wanted to be. And that set him, and us, on a different path. He changed. Don't get me wrong; he took a lot of crap from a lot of people for 'going backwards.' His dad talking about all the money they invested in him to go to med school. His mom made sarcastic comments at holiday dinners about how she almost had a doctor in the family. But I'm proud of Tom for being true to himself. Change is always possible. So, whatever doubts you are having about starting over and going after something you truly want, you should remove them and just go for it."

Tom added, "Brian, it's never too late for a new beginning. My clients and a large percentage of the people running the marathon today are doing so because they need to prove something to themselves. Somewhere along the way in their lives, they stopped learning and growing. They stopped making good choices for themselves. They sacrificed their well-being day by day, forgoing their mental or physical health, or a new experience, because they fell into a rut they couldn't get out of. They can't quit their jobs. They don't want to quit their relationships. But they have lost control of their lives. They tried eating, drinking, gambling, reality TV . . . basically any form of escape they could think of to mask the pain of not being the person they thought they would be when they got to 'this' age. Then, one day they woke up with a need to shock their own system. They finally said, 'Damn it. I'm going to run a marathon,' and prove to themselves that they could still exceed even their own expectations. They made the commitment to train for it and go for it, because if you don't train for it, you'll die at mile number six. All my clients made the commitment and then built up their skill and stamina each day. Little by little, they added more to their mileage, and when they started seeing results, they started eating better and sleeping more. They took their image, their health, and even the relationship they had with themselves more personally. They felt more alive at work and at home. They didn't need to escape anymore, because they were living their best life.

"For me, I see it every day. As a personal trainer, it's my job to help someone make every decision the right one and take every action personally."

Brian thought about running a marathon a few years ago. But that's as far as it went. He thought about it. The idea of it sounded great. He and Jen talked about doing it together, but that was before kids and before all the extra layers of stress. So he would have a Bloody Mary and watch the marathon every year instead. That's the difference between successful people and those who want to be successful. There are some who have great ideas but don't follow through, and those who have good ideas but execute to the end. A good idea executed is always better than a brilliant idea that stays just an idea.

Tara added, "As I tell all of my high potentials and executives at work, building and maintaining a brand is like a marathon. Once you make a commitment to it, you have to follow through. You have to be consistent in your actions, over time, if you want to see great results."

"Start a task. Finish a task," Tom blurted.

"You always use my line." Tara rolled her eyes.

"Yeah," Tom answered, "why wouldn't I use your line? Start a task. Finish a task. There is no greater, simpler line than that. If you commit to something that will build or strengthen your brand, you have to see it through. Whether it's physical, mental, emotional, or spiritual, you have to be consistent in your actions. Your reputation is who you are and what you do. But, ultimately, people recognize you for your results and what you see through to the end."

Brian thought about all of the things he started but never finished. He thought about what his life might be like if he finished all the tasks he began.

Tara continued, "Brian, you have to unsubscribe from all the things that could possibly push your brand off track. It's *decision management.* To decide means literally 'to kill off.' When you decide, you kill off all other potential options. When I decided to marry Tom, I decided he was the one. I said, 'I will forgo all others for this one man.' I literally said there are no other options. That is the power of a decision. Anytime you are forced to choose, you don't have to pick the best option. You just have to kill off all the other options that are not going to improve your life."

"She's tried to kill me off a few times," Tom laughed.

"That's not true," Tara added. "If I wanted him killed, he'd be dead already."

Brian smiled, wondering how his own wife currently thought about her decision to marry him.

"It's about ROA," Tara continued.

"ROA?" Brian asked.

Tara said, "Return on actions. You've heard of ROI, Return on investments. Well, both Tom and I, when we talk with our different kinds of clients, focus on ROA and how people need to invest in themselves. Tom focuses on transformation of mind, body, and spirit. I focus on transformation and enhancement of skills and talents. In either case, we train our clients to invest in themselves, and know every action is either going to bring them closer to, or further away from, their goals. So, you have to assess every potential action as an investment of your time and energy. Is it a good investment, and what will you get out of it?"

Tom added, "There's only four kinds of actions when you are talking about creating or strengthening your reputation, Brian. You can be **proactive, reactive, distractive,** or **destructive**. That's it. Most people are reactive. They do their jobs, and when someone needs something, they get it done. Reactive. But, great brands are more than that. People need to think of themselves as brand managers; really think about every aspect of your work and life as a brand. Think proactively about standing out among your colleagues and competitors, and plan out a course of action to get there. Those are the people who usually rise to the top.

"For the people who are distractive or destructive, well, that's like texting while driving. You keep taking your eyes off the road, just like taking your eyes off your life or your career, and you will eventually crash. No one is responsible for your reputation and the recognition you receive except you."

Tara added, "Don't make decisions, Brian. Make commitments. Make commitments to your family, to your career, but most importantly, commit to yourself. Commitments are decisions based on values and beliefs."

Tom smiled at Tara.

"I just love this woman when she talks about behavior modification."

Brian thought of his wife. He thought of how she stuck by him when he was feeling 'less than.' She pumped him up, even when the job got him down. But now he realized that wasn't fair to her. It was up to him to own his own reputation and be accountable for the strength of it. It was up to him to be consistent in his values and words and actions. He was the only one accountable for the success or failure of his career.

He might not have committed to running a marathon, but at that moment, he committed to something far more important. He committed to stop waiting for his wife, his future boss, or anyone else to make him feel valued. It was up to him and him alone to feel valued by creating value.

Tom finished, "Brian, we are going to run out to the street to see a few more of our folks in action. They are running for time, so I just want to be there to give them some encouragement. So please hold our seats. But there's one thing I'd like to say, before the day becomes a madhouse and we don't have a chance to talk further. You are born, and someone has hopes and dreams for you. They imagine the possibilities of what you could become. But it has to be about your dreams. Be consistent. Be resilient. Even when you are not at your best, you must remember to be the best version of yourself possible for that day. When you make the right decisions, and take the right actions based on the right beliefs, you have the power to change everything. Never forget that."

Brian survived the day and the night shift that followed. As expected, he made more money in those 14 hours than he had in the previous three shifts. It was a good day for his bank account, but an even better day for his future.

16 Flow

Seven weeks behind the bar and Brian was incredibly comfortable. Not only was he a better bartender, but Tara Traynor was right; he was becoming a better person.

He was meeting many wonderful people who would share their stories of second chances with him, but he also met a number of people who were very unhappy with their jobs and unwilling to do anything about it, except complain.

Brian was curious about happiness, and with *experience* as his aspirational brand, he wanted to know more. He decided to ask the seemingly happy people where and how they found their joy. The answers were always the same. They felt challenged. They felt a sense of purpose. They felt like they had a particular set of skills and were using their talents to make a difference in the world. One patron even gave Brian a copy of the book *Flow* by psychologist Mihaly Csikszentmihalyi, who wrote about the creation of "optimal experience." The author said that what makes an experience genuinely satisfying is a state of consciousness called *flow*. During flow, people typically experience deep enjoyment, creativity, and a total involvement with work and life. Brian was taken aback when he discovered the six factors that encompassed an optimal "flow" experience:

1. An intense and focused concentration on the present moment.

2. The merging of action and awareness.

3. A loss of self-consciousness.

4. A sense of personal control over a situation or activity.

5. One's experience of time is altered.

6. Experience of the activity is intrinsically rewarding.

As Brian thought about his previous job and his jobs before that, he couldn't help but think about "flow" and the lack of it he had. He was never focused on the present. Always worried about the future. Watching the clock. He was always self-conscious about what this boss or his colleagues thought about him. He never felt in control of any situation, always having to answer to someone or get approval from someone. He always felt like every minute of every day was just there to torture him, and he certainly didn't feel any joy in his job where it felt like it was intrinsically rewarding. The job was a paycheck.

As he reflected on his almost two months behind the bar, he thought about creating optimal experiences, not only for himself, but for others. As his skills increased and he was able to create a better experience for his patrons, he took account-ability for the quality of their experience. In doing so, his own experience at work began to change, and he was, in his own evaluation, experiencing flow. The hours flew by, altering the perception of time, even in the late hours. He was only in the present, aware of everything around him. He was in control of everyone's experience, providing great service, and at the end of the night, felt like he made a difference in helping people get happier. Not a bad way to make a buck. But was it possible to translate that kind of work into a long-term career?

With three weeks before his temporary run at Crossroads was over, he began to narrow his focus to industries and jobs where the value he could provide, based on his present and potential future skills, would create an optimal experience for himself and his future customers. Like the bartending, he knew that whatever he wanted to do in the future might not come easy at first, but he was no longer afraid to be uncomfortable, work hard, or to be challenged to become the best possible version of himself.

17 Protect the Business, Protect the Brand

It was a Saturday night, and Brian spotted trouble from the start. The tall man with the slicked-back hair at the back of the crowd was not going to wait his turn to get up to the bar, and Brian could see the other patrons becoming visibly annoyed as the man pushed his way to the middle of the crowd. The music was loud. The crowd was loud. Brian was moving as quickly as possible to get to everyone who wanted a drink. He prided himself on being more aware of not just the customer in front of him, but the entire crowd. He liked to think of it as his customer vision shifting from tunnel to panoramic. He smiled to himself as he thought about how he would tell Jack to use that as a topic for one of his TIPs.

Brian's smile quickly faded when he saw the troublemaker trying to plow his way through a group of women politely waiting their turn to order a drink. The tall man didn't realize that one of the women was standing next to her boyfriend. That boyfriend was big and didn't take kindly to the pushing of his girl, nor did he appreciate the words that the trouble-maker used to describe her, when she told the man to stop pushing.

Loud words were exchanged, and Brian could see a fight was about to happen. Sure enough, the boyfriend pushed the troublemaker, which moved the entire crowd a few feet backward. The tall man was about to lunge back at the boyfriend, with his arm cocked back, ready to throw a punch. But he never got the chance.

Brian, sensing potential for a melee, and without thinking, swiftly pulled himself up onto the beer cooler and then in one motion stepped onto the bar and threw himself into the middle of the action like a rock star attempting to surf the crowd at a concert. However, he landed on his feet and grabbed the troublemaker from behind, pinning his arms behind his head in a full nelson, and pushed him all the way through the crowd and out the front door. Brian told the bouncers not to let the tall man in the rest of the night. Of course, the troublemaker had a few choice words for Brian, but Brian didn't care. He was already on his way back into the bar and made his way back to his station.

There was applause from the crowd and a quick hand-shake from the boyfriend.

"Thanks for that!" the boyfriend shouted.

"My pleasure," Brian responded.

It actually was his pleasure. Brian had not been in a fight or even put his hands on another person since eighth grade. His heart was pounding, and he felt incredible. He could have waited for the bouncers to step in once the fight started, but he knew that would disrupt the crowd and the evening. It may have escalated, and someone could have gotten hurt. What if the cops came and the whole evening went to hell? He could try to rationalize it, but the truth was he made a split decision to make sure no one got hurt. It could have gone differently, but he felt he made the right move.

The boyfriend ordered a round for his crowd and handed Brian an extra $20 as a tip.

"You made sure tonight didn't go wrong, 'cause that guy was about to go down, and I probably would have been taken out of here in handcuffs."

"Yeah, I could tell it wasn't going to be a friendly discussion," Brian laughed.

The boyfriend turned back to his group, and Brian looked down the bar towards Kelly. She pointed at him, made a fist, and pounded her chest, as if to say, "respect."

From that point on, the night was business as usual. No fights. No altercations. Just lots of people, lots of drinks, and a heck of a lot of tips. It was about three hours later when the crowd started to thin out and Brian began cleaning up his station.

The boyfriend returned to order a final round for his friends.

"So, do you do that often?" he asked.

"Do what?" Brian responded.

"Jump the bar like that. It's a risky move. I would have said you had about a 40% chance of getting over the bar, landing properly, securing that dude, and getting him out of the bar without getting hurt, or getting hit."

Brian smiled. "It was my first time. I wasn't really thinking."

"Well in that case, now knowing you never did that before, I'd have given you a 20% chance of coming away clean." The boyfriend extended his hand. "I'm Kurt."

"I'm Brian. Are you a bookie, Kurt?"

"Ha. That's funny. Actually, not a bookie, but I guess you could think of what I do as odds-making. I'm a risk manager."

Brian continued to wipe down the bottles in his station.

"Risk manager. What's that?"

"Well, typically risk managers assess and identify potential risks to an organization that could hinder reputation, safety, security, or financial stability. I identify those risks and work with the right people in my organization to develop a strategy that reduces the severity and/or probability of that risk."

"Sounds interesting. So, were you thinking about your own risk when you shoved that jerk?"

"Good point. No. Not my own risk. I was thinking about the risk to my girlfriend and her friends. My goal was to move the risk away from them. Technically, that's what I do at work as well. I transfer risk away from my company."

"So, what kind of risk is the most dangerous for a company."

"Well, I work for an underground construction company."

"That sounds dangerous."

"It is. Under our feet, below our lakes, rivers, and oceans, run utility lines, tunnels, and structures. If you hit one of the utility lines, it can kill you, and sometimes everyone around you. Gas, propane, and electricity all have the potential to destroy. So, if you ask me what the greatest risk to a company is, I'd have to say it's the people."

"The people?"

"Yup. The people. Most companies fail because of people. Most accidents happen because of people. Most reputations are destroyed because of people. A business's good name and reputation is worth more than 75% of an organization's value. If a company loses value it's because the people fail to follow through on the promise that the company stands for.

"In my company, if my people don't follow guidelines, people die. In hospitals, if people don't follow proper procedures, people die, and the hospital gets sued. In financial institutions, if people don't follow ethical guidelines, people don't die, but reputations do. So, I always like to say that my company is like any company. There are unseen risks that can become destructive at any moment, and it's up to me, and my fellow risk managers, to minimize the risk or the impact of those destructive behaviors.

"I always remind people that you are never not a representative of your company and the company brand. No matter where you are, on the clock or off the clock, your reputation is a direct connection to the company and everyone in that company. So, you are accountable for your own future, but when you are part of a company or team, you are accountable for everyone's future as well."

Brian thought about risk and reputation and realized that in any company, and on any team, the reputation of the team is only as strong as the weakest individual.

"I work with people in all departments of my company, and everyone is most worried about alignment. Are the people aligned? Do they understand why we are in business, and what their role is in keeping that business operating and thriving? Every person is an integral part of the organization, and if one person refuses to protect the business and the brand, then the company is at risk. For me it's about consistent quality, safety, and compliance. I work to protect the company brand."

Brian knew that jumping the bar was probably a stupid idea. He put himself at risk for injury, but not doing anything would have put the bar at greater risk. What if a fight broke out and a bottle was broken and someone got badly hurt? Who would be responsible? The bar probably had insurance, but what kind of insurance? And, even if it covered a lawsuit, wouldn't a serious injury prevent people from coming back to the establishment? All it takes is one event and one moment to change everything. So, he did what he thought was best for "his company," which upon further reflection was not something he would have done just a few months ago. He felt a sense of duty to protect the business and the brand.

"People are the most valuable asset of any organization. Which is why I tend to work a lot with Talent Development and Human Resources. In my company we invest time and money to hire, train, and engage our entire workforce. If an employee is engaged and feels the company stands with them as much as the employee stands for the company, that's alignment, and that can be very powerful. Organizations want people who are going to consistently represent their brand and minimize their exposure to risk. So, if they hire people who live and breathe the culture and the values, then they know those people will fulfill the promise of the company to their customers."

"I'm between jobs at the moment," Brian stated. "I'm working here temporarily, and I've been thinking about what new kind of career I want, and how I'm supposed to support and protect my family. I'd hop the bar for them just as easily as I did tonight. So, I guess you could say I'm looking for a company that feels like family."

Kurt smiled. "Yeah. There are a lot of great companies out there that know how to take care of the people that take care of their brand. Keep looking. You'll find it. And when you do, just make sure they know how much protecting their business and their brand means to you. If you can show that, they'll be scrambling to bring you into their world."

Brian shook the risk manager's hand and thanked him for the advice. Protect the business and the brand like you'd protect your family. Hop the bar if necessary. Minimize or transfer the risk and exposure. Do that and you'll always have an employer that values you. Good advice for any employee.

18 Day of All Days

Two weeks left at Crossroads, but Sunday was not going to be about an interview or a job or a career or how many vodka tonics he was going to make. Sunday was his son's birthday.

The day started with balloons. Birthdays in the Davis house always start with balloons. Jen likes to think that she started the tradition of having balloons waiting for the kids in the kitchen when they wake up in the morning, but in reality, it was Brian who started the balloon thing by filling their first apartment with balloons on Jen's birthday long before they had kids. She came home from work one night to find the whole place covered in multicolored balloons. She smiled for days. He was a hero.

When the kids came along and he was focused more on working and making money, he left the "creating experiences" job to Jen. Another muscle that he stopped exercising until it atrophied. He would show up for the parties and family gatherings, and every once in a while would offer input on which cousin should sit next to which cousin at the family holidays, but for the most part Jen was the event planner in the family, and she was really good at it. Why stick his nose into the process?

Drew was into dinosaurs. What six-year-old wasn't? So, what better place to have a birthday than at the Museum of Natural History? Twenty kids and a few parents. It was a great idea, and best of all, it wasn't at his house, so he didn't have to clean up the mess.

Jen made sure to reserve a group tour designed for young children, and the tour guide they had was exceptional. The guide knew what a group of six-year-olds would want to see and spoke to them in a way that was educational, inspiring, and fun. She told stories and engaged the entire group in a way that made each child feel special. It was an extra cost to have the guide, but Jen believed it would be worth it to have someone who could enhance the experience and make it memorable beyond the cake and presents.

It was a perfect day, and when it was over, the Davis family made it back to the house in time for Drew to open all his presents, take a bath, and get ready for bed.

"How was your day?" Brian asked his son.

Drew smiled. "I liked the T-Rex."

"Me too. Pretty cool, right?"

"Uh-huh."

"I'm glad you had a good day, but it's time for bed. Which book?"

Jen and Brian always read to the kids. Story time at night was a great way to settle the troops, create routines, reduce stress, and even help them sleep better. Studies also suggested that reading to kids before bed every night would build vocabulary, cultivate imagination, and foster a love of reading on their own. If Brian wanted to know where any of the extra money he made over the past six years was, all he had to do was look at the floor-to-ceiling bookshelves in his kids' rooms.

Drew reached over the side of his bed and pulled up his book.

"Sammy gave me this one today, 'cause it's my birthday."

It was the Dr. Seuss book *Happy Birthday to You!*

Brian knew that even the reading of a book out loud was the creation of an experience. He could just read, or he could perform and create something memorable.

"Okay, here we go."

Brian began reading about the Great Birthday Bird, who swoops in on your birthday and creates a phenomenal experience for you on the Day of all Days. Brian was staying in character. He was taking on the persona of the Great Birthday Bird as he read every word, and Drew loved the performance.

Brian was surprised how much it was a message for anyone who needed to be reminded that being you is enough. We spend so much time beating ourselves up for being what we're not, he thought, that we forget to just be the best us. The very wise Dr. Seuss strikes again.

They finished the book, and Brian gave Drew a hug and kiss goodnight.

"Dad?" Drew asked.

"Yeah, bud?"

"I'm glad I'm me."

"I'm glad you're you, too."

Brian put the new book on the bookshelf and shut the light, leaving the door open just a crack so there was a bit of light streaming into the room.

Brian went downstairs and met Jen in the kitchen.

"Long day." She let out a deep breath.

"Great day," he responded.

She smiled.

"You're different these days."

"Different how?"

"More you."

"What does that mean?"

"Not sure. Just, more you. It's a good thing," she assured him.

He chuckled.

"You were always you," she added. "You're just more . . . you . . . now. I don't care about the house or the stuff. And the kids are resilient. I want you to be happy. I want us to be happy. Whether you stay and keep doing what you're doing, or find something else, or I find something and you stay home, don't settle for something that makes you less than you. I don't like that guy. I really like this guy."

He pulled her in close for a hug.

He knew they would be okay. He knew he would find something that allowed him to feel lucky to be his true self. He just hoped it was soon, otherwise they'd be out of savings and living month to month.

As the two of them began to straighten up the house before going to bed, Brian checked his e-mails on the phone. There was one from a name he didn't recognize with the subject header, "Opportunity for a meeting." He clicked it open.

Hello Mr. Davis—

My name is Cara Crenshaw, and I just had a very interesting conversation with a colleague of mine who knows you from Crossroads. They think you might be the perfect person for a role I'm trying to fill within my organization. I am setting up interviews this week and would like to know if you are available to meet for an introduction to see if this is something that might interest you. I have attached the description of the role and an overview of our organization. Please take a look and get back to me as soon as possible.

Warm Regards,

Cara

Brian clicked open the attachment and smiled. Maybe this really was the day of all days.

19 Create an Experience

Three days later, Brian arrived at the hotel 15 minutes early. The bellman greeted him with a friendly hello as he walked into the building.

He entered the lobby and looked around. It was obvious why the hotel was rated five stars by *Forbes*, and five diamonds by AAA. He had done his research not only on the hotel but also the entire hotel group, which had locations in all the major cities in the United States, as well as international properties and resorts throughout Canada, Europe, Asia-Pacific, Central America, and the Caribbean. It was a luxury brand that catered to sophisticated leisure and business travelers looking for memorable experiences. It was welcoming from the entry, all the way up the marble staircase to the reception area.

Cara Crenshaw was the Regional VP of sales and marketing for the hotel group, and upon a quick LinkedIn search, when he got her e-mail, Brian could see that she had been in the hospitality industry for most of her life. He was supposed to meet her at 2:00 p.m. in the Downtown Ballroom on the third floor. He was surprised he wasn't meeting Cara in her office or an interview room of some kind, but he just assumed she was busy and trying to multitask.

He pulled open the large mahogany door of the ballroom and entered. The room looked like it was set for a wedding or a very elaborate awards dinner. There were about 30 tables covered with white tablecloths and beautiful flowers. Individual menus were at each place setting, and the number 100 was everywhere, including the backdrop behind the stage at the front of the room.

He spotted the one person in the room sitting up at the front table, near the stage, which had yet to be set with any silverware. Just a clean white tablecloth.

"Good afternoon!" he said loud enough to be heard from the back of the room.

"Brian? Please come in and join me here at the table," the woman responded.

They shook hands, and Brian sat down at the table, putting his computer bag on the seat next to him. Cara Crenshaw was probably in her late forties and exuded the qualities of the brand she represented. Her entire appearance from her clothes, to her hair, and even her posture was the hotel brand personified, sophisticated and elegant.

"Thank you for coming in today," she started. "I have to tell you, when I hire, I usually look within the industry at people who have years of experience. But my colleague said I'd be foolish not to bring you in for a conversation."

"Who is your colleague?" Brian asked.

"Tracy," she responded.

Brian thought for a moment. "Super Premium Tracy? The liquor rep?"

Cara smiled. "That's the one. Gave her my account two years ago, and she never lets me down. She said she met you on the first day you worked at Crossroads and has watched your transformation. She said you are a natural for the hospitality industry."

Brian smiled. "Well, I'll admit, at first I wasn't sure how the whole bartending thing was going to turn out, but I guess you could say that I've embraced the idea of helping people get happier."

"That's great. So how would you like to get out from behind the bar, and help people create shared experiences that foster collaboration and connection? I'm looking for someone who understands the corporate world, sales, world-class customer service, and the importance of face-to-face human interaction. Tracy seems to think you have all that. You got the description of the role I sent, yes?"

He nodded. It was a corporate sales position focused on selling the hotel's meeting and guest room space to organizations looking to hold high-profile meetings and events for their most important internal and external audiences. His responsibilities would consist of developing and nurturing relationships with existing corporate accounts, as well as prospecting and securing new accounts that aligned with the marketing and sales strategy set forth by the global sales division. He would report directly to Cara, but have to work across the divisions to make sure the hotel exceeded client expectations.

"Yes, I received the description."

This was a company and a brand he would be proud to work for.

She nodded. "I brought you into this room because I wanted to show you what you have to work with. Your product is this hotel and all the space from top to bottom. The quality of our food, people, and location is exceptional. Tonight, there will be 200 people here to celebrate the 100-million-dollar mark for their company. Hence the number 100 everywhere. It's a milestone for them, and they are bringing everyone together, and spending a nice chunk of their profits, to show all 200 employees the importance of a shared experience. They are bringing in a well-known band and a very expensive motivational speaker. No expense will be spared. This is their night, and they want every moment to be exceptional. This is what we do. Every day and every evening. Actually, 24/7. We are a luxury brand, which means only the best will do. Do you think you can bring that kind of energy, Brian? Because here, no one is allowed to have a bad day. Not even me."

Brian nodded.

"So, why should I take a chance on you, Brian? Tell me what Tracy saw in you that makes you a good fit here."

Brian was about to explain how he was a loyal and dedicated employee. But he knew that's not what Cara wanted to hear. If he was going to sell experiences, he'd have to create one. He looked in front of him, and there was a stage. It would be used that evening for an awards ceremony and a band and a speaker. It was time to make the most of the environment.

He got up from the table and jumped up onto the stage. He remembered how Kelly jumped up onto the bar and told him to "bring it." It was a bold move, and judging by the surprised look on Cara's face, he wasn't sure if it was going to work. But he wasn't going to leave the interview without knowing he'd given everything he had.

"Wow!" he screamed.

Cara jumped a little bit in her seat.

"Wow!" he screamed it again. "Such a great word. But, what is WOW? What makes you say it, feel it, live it? You ask me if I have the energy to represent this brand? I say YES, because while I thought my personal brand could be defined by the word *experience*, I realized the moment I entered this hotel lobby that experience isn't enough to be part of this company and this brand. People won't walk into this room and want just an experience. People want . . . WOW!

"They want to be wowed by the environment. They want to walk in this place and have their jaws drop because it's like nothing they've ever seen before. They want WOW food. The kind that makes you have to put the fork down and say, 'Oh my goodness, Cara, you have to try this. It's the most amazing thing you will ever taste in your life!' They want WOW service. The kind that makes you say, 'they must be able to read my mind because I was thinking it . . . and then it happened.'

"If you could describe me and my purpose in one word, Cara, that word would be . . . WOW. Three letters that launch me out of bed in the morning because I know that my purpose in life is to help people experience WOW in their own lives. That's who I am, and it's what I will do every single day for you and for this organization. I will make your job easier, because I know this job is not about selling a room. It's about selling the potential of a memory that lasts a lifetime.

It's about making a difference in someone's life, not just that day, but every day after that day. It's about creating new connections that change the world. WOW is about creating stories that people retell over and over again because it's too good of a story not to be told.

"So, while I didn't see it on your website, or read it in your mission statement, I know that this company, this hotel, and your team exist to create WOW. You, personally, are here to create WOW. As someone who would represent you, and this hotel, and this global brand, you can be assured I will never ever have a bad day. I will bring the WOW every single day, and that's why I belong here!"

He stopped speaking. He stopped moving. He might have even been a little out of breath. *Where did that come from?* he thought to himself. It wasn't planned. He didn't rehearse it. WOW? Where did he pull that word from? He didn't even know there would be a stage. He just knew it had to be said, because it's what he felt, and he knew that even if Cara told him he was crazy and to get out of the room and never come back, he knew in his own moment of WOW, he finally found his word, his purpose, and possibly even his future career. He wasn't lying or exaggerating. From that moment on, he would never have a bad day again.

Cara stared at him, but didn't say a word. Maybe she was too shocked to speak, or maybe she knew he needed to catch his breath. But, eventually, she did speak.

"Wow," she said.

"Wow," he repeated.

She picked up her cell phone and dialed.

"Tracy ... Bring that extra case of super premium scotch tomorrow. You win. He's hired."

She looked up at Brian.

"When can you start?" she asked.

20 The Last TIP

Brian's last night at Crossroads felt like a party. It was a Friday night, and all the regulars, throughout the evening, made their way to the middle of the bar to shake his hand and wish him well on his new job. He didn't have time to talk with many of them for long, because the place was packed, but he made sure to thank everyone for their support throughout the 10 weeks. Jimmy would be coming back the next week, and Brian would be starting his new career on Monday morning. Some of the regulars even told Brian they thought he was better than Jimmy, and they would be sorry to see him go. He liked hearing that.

It was a crazy week and a half since Cara made him the offer on the spot. Of course, he said yes without even hearing what the compensation would be. He didn't care. He knew it was the right role and the right company for him. Turns out, the base pay was better than what he had at his last job, the commission structure was generous, and even the benefits were better. Plus, he would be immediately enrolled in the leadership development program, since they looked to promote from within the company, all the way to the executive level.

But, to top it off, after Brian filled out all the paperwork, and the background check was completed, and his employment was official, Cara called him with a surprise. The hotel wasn't going to be busy on Wednesday night, and if he wasn't doing anything, would he and his family like to stay at the hotel for the evening . . . in the presidential suite? Maybe show the family where he would be working?

When they got to the hotel, the staff gave him and his family the complete VIP treatment. The kids thought they were in a castle, and the suite was as big as their entire house. Cara made sure to stop by and say hello to Jen and the kids, explaining that if Brian was going to sell the WOW experience, he should know what it felt like, as the customer.

She also knew that by bringing his whole family to experience what his "product" would be like, Cara allowed him to be the hero, to his kids . . . even for one night.

"You get to work here every day?!"

For that, he would be forever grateful to Cara and his new company. Isn't that what anyone wants? To come home from work and know that your family respects you and the work you do? To be the hero? And that night in the hotel, after the kids swam in the pool, ran up and down the hallways, danced in the lobby, gorged themselves on room service, and watched pay-per-view movies, vowing to never leave, they all fell into a deep sleep on 500-thread count Egyptian cotton sheets. It was an escape . . . a fantasy . . . a WOW experience . . . and he would get to sell it every day.

His last night of mayhem at Crossroads. He would miss it. Talking to people from all walks of life. It allowed him to get out of his lane and learn more about what really makes people happier. Sure, the alcohol had something to do with it. But you can go to the store and buy a whole bottle of alcohol and drink it at home with your friends for a fraction of what you spend at a bar or restaurant. No, if it were just about the booze, there wouldn't be so many places where people leave the comfort of their homes to sit or stand in a crowded room with strangers and pay four times the cost. People crave interaction and experiences. He once again remembered the conversation he overheard a few weeks back. The only differences between you today and you a year from now are the new things you read, the new people you meet, and the new experiences you have. If you don't learn or experience new things, you don't grow.

If Brian learned anything in his 10 weeks at Crossroads, it was to never underestimate the power of human interaction and experience. He was different, and it felt amazing.

Just then, he saw Tracy enter the bar. He hadn't seen her since he got the new job. He had called her at the number on her business card, but she didn't answer, so he left a message of thanks. She made her way to the bar, and Brian grabbed her hand since he couldn't reach over and hug her.

"Congratulations!" she said.

"I can't thank you enough," Brian said. "It's the perfect job."

"For you, it will be. That's why I recommended you."

"Seriously, though. Why would you put your own reputation on the line for someone you don't even know?"

"Do you remember my purpose statement?" she asked.

"Something about top shelf …"

"I help people make top-shelf decisions in work and life by always providing super premium products, service, thinking, and partnership. Cara is my client. I am her collaborative partner. I don't just sell spirits. She's always asked me to keep my eyes open for a certain kind of talent and experience. I didn't know you that well, but I saw how quickly you took to this place, and how you made customer service your priority, and the fact that you had a corporate sales background. You were the top-shelf person she was looking for, so I just made the intro."

"You changed my life," he said.

"No," she answered, "you changed your life. I would have never put my reputation on the line if I didn't believe you were the right person for the job."

He smiled. "What can I get you? It's on the house. Super premium?"

"Always."

The night went quickly. Brian was once again in a state of flow, and as the crowd started to thin out hours later, and the volume of the music was turned down, Jack and Kelly began to clean up. An hour later, the bar was closed. Jack locked the front doors while Brian and Kelly sat down at a table along the back wall of the lounge area with the three tip buckets full of money. It was a familiar routine.

"I remember the first night you worked here," Kelly laughed.

"I remember too," Brian added. "Wasn't pretty. And I wasn't all that valuable either. If I remember, I think you called me a drunk monkey."

"No, I said I think a drunk monkey would be able to make more money than you did."

"And break less glasses and bottles," Brian added. "Yeah, I remember."

"You've come a long way," Kelly added.

"Thanks," he replied.

Jack entered the room and flopped himself down in one of the chairs. "So, how'd we do?"

"Could be a record night for us," Kelly said. "The WOW man over here was pulling in all the goodbye tips tonight."

"WOW man. I kind of like that," Brian laughed.

"The name's a little dorky," Jack interjected. "We'll have to work on that. But it's appropriate because in any great story, there has to be a hero who overcomes adversity and transforms into a better version of himself. You got fired, Brian. But you stepped up to the challenge, and now look at you. I guarantee you'll be running that hotel soon enough."

"Couldn't have done it without you both," Brian added.

"Seriously, are we gonna get all mushy here? Sure, we'll miss you, but you can come crosstown for a drink once in a while. It's not like you're going to another country," Kelly said.

Brian smiled. "Maybe I could even guest bartend here once in a while. Help out if you need it."

"Maybe," Jack said.

They counted the tips, and it was, in fact, the best night they ever had, and that included their nights with Jimmy. Brian was no longer a stand-in or a placeholder, and he vowed never to be one again.

Kelly grabbed her tips and gave Brian a hug goodbye.

"It was great working with you. I wish you all the best. I better get a discount when I come to that fancy place of yours after I land my hit TV show."

"You can count on it," Brian said.

As she left out the back door, Brian picked up his share of the tip money.

"Before you leave," Jack said, "I wanted to give you something."

Jack grabbed a large glass mason jar and slid it in front of Brian.

"You're giving me a dirty glass. Umm . . . thank you?"

"I'm giving you something to remind you to take it personally. When you first came here, that first night we sat back here counting tips, I explained to you why I feel so strongly about my definition of TIP. Tips are not something you get, they are the result of something you give."

"I remember," Brian said.

"Every night you were here, we started the night with three empty tip buckets. And, every night by the end of the night they were overflowing with bills. Singles. Fives. Tens. Twenties. Even hundreds from time to time. All those tips added up. And by the end of the night we were able to look at the total and declare whether we had a good night or not and whether we provided value to our customers. Agreed?"

"Agreed."

Brian could sense an analogy coming. Jack loved analogies.

"So, I want you to keep this glass jar as a symbol for the way to approach your new career and your new life. Every day you wake up, think of the glass as empty, and it's your job to fill it with your own tips, so by the end of the day you can determine if you added value to someone's world. Ten weeks ago, I remember you saying that you wished you had a tip jar on your desk so if anyone asked you to do anything and you did it, they would throw money into your jar. You said that would be motivating. What did I say?"

"You said that was external motivation," Brian answered.

"Exactly. And, no one ever got super successful by just being externally motivated. So, keep your personal tip jar on your desk or somewhere in your office, or wherever. But instead of expecting someone else to fill it, do it yourself. When you give more, you get more. You are going to make more sales than you ever have in your life. When you get a sale, that's a tip in your jar because you gave more. When you get a promotion or a raise, that's a tip in your jar because you worked more. When you win an award or get recognition from your boss or peers or industry, that's a tip in your jar because you cared more. When you bring an idea to the table that no one else thought of, and it gets implemented, that's a tip in your jar because you innovated more. You see what I'm saying?"

"Yes. I'm responsible for the value of my tip jar."

"Absolutely. Fill that jar with words and actions that will add value to others. When you look inside that glass jar, you will see everything you've accomplished to create a career, and a life, of lasting success."

Brian thought for a moment.

"So, your jar is your brand. It's your reputation."

Jack nodded. "It's who you are, what you say, what you do and who you help."

Brian continued. "And everything I put into it, I'll get out of it."

"And all the results and recognition you get will be because you gave more."

Jack took a dollar bill from his cut of the tips that evening and put it on the table. He then pulled out a black marker and took the cap off. He wrote "Take It Personally" on the back of the bill and put it into Brian's new glass tip jar.

"Here's your last TIP at Crossroads. You're about to embark on a new journey for yourself and your family. Don't think about the money you get. Think about the value you'll give. Come back from time to time and visit. Come celebrate when you get your big sales or promotions. Come celebrate when you buy a new house, or whatever it is that feels like a milestone in your life. Come back if you need a reminder of who you are, even in the tough times. Because there will always be tough times. But I'm predicting tonight is your last night here. It's time to move on."

Brian thought back to a few months ago when every day he felt fearful and worried. No job to go to. No friends who could help. No understanding of how to start over. But tonight, armed with a new set of tools to create the career of a lifetime, he felt hope and excitement. Go into the world and see what you can do if you put everything you have into each day. Don't let a moment go by when you are not trying to fill that tip jar with proof that you are fulfilling the promise you make to yourself, your family, your team, and your company.

"Come on," Jack said, "I'll let you out the front door."

Brian grabbed his tips and his glass jar and made his way to the front of Crossroads. He gave Jack a hug and thanked him again for everything.

"Keep sending me those e-mail TIPs," Brian said.

"Of course." Jack nodded and closed and locked the door behind him.

Brian stood outside for a moment and looked up at the Crossroads sign. Two paths interconnected. At one time it might have meant uncertainty. Which path is the right path? Now standing alone on the sidewalk with no one else around, he saw the interconnection as opportunity, endless opportunity where every decision and every path taken is the right path, as long as you stay true and stay you.

Present Day

21 The TIP Jar (Continued)

Brian sat at his desk, holding the glass tip jar and remembering how he had felt standing outside Crossroads that evening, 12 years earlier. Opportunity. That, he concluded, was the difference maker in his career. He looked at every decision as an opportunity to either prove the value he had, or learn a new skill to upgrade the value he could bring.

Today would be another crossroads in his life. A chance to take on a new challenge. He wasn't a perfect candidate for the CEO role, just like his first job with the company. He had qualities that someone saw as valuable, qualities that would be the foundation for something more. As he moved up the ranks of the organization, and started to hire his own people, he remembered to hire for attitude. Hire for potential value. We can train. We can add the technical skills. Hire the hungry. Hire those with something to prove.

He thought about that first job. He was so hungry that first day he walked into the hotel in midtown as a corporate sales manager. He vowed never to take a growth opportunity for granted. Whatever it took, he would do it . . . and he did.

No one rose through the company as fast as he did. Some would say he should have waited his turn. Others in the organization had more experience and paid their dues. And who the heck was he to even be in the running for CEO? But Brian didn't care. He wasn't there to make friends with people who put politics over performance and purpose. He was there to add value. And if people saw him as a threat, then maybe they weren't working hard or smart enough. He learned to promote himself even before his titles changed. In his mind, the title promotion was the TIP he received after giving all of himself all the time.

Put it in the jar. Every win. Every compliment. Every newspaper article where he was quoted. Every award he received, either for himself or on behalf of the organization. Every raise or bonus. Every person who said, "I want to work with you, or for you." It all went into the jar. TIPs for giving more of himself.

Brian kept his promise. He would come back to Crossroads every time there was a milestone or promotion in his life. He came in when he made his first sale, just two weeks into the new job. He came in when he took over Cara Crenshaw's job two years later, when she relocated to an international position. He came in when he was accepted to a weekend graduate school program to get his MBA, and he came in when he finally graduated a few years later. He celebrated a little extra hard that night because finance wasn't the easiest thing for him.

He pushed himself. If he wanted to grow within the organization, he had to be uncomfortable from time to time and push himself to be the best version of himself. When he was given more international responsibilities and was eventually made head of global sales and marketing, Brian brought his entire team into Crossroads to celebrate.

He took advantage of every opportunity, and it served him well. At first, he would ask himself if he was even worthy of putting his name in the hat for certain positions. But then he realized that any time you get the chance to move up, you are going to be in a place you've never been before. And when that happens you just have to remember that you are going "break a few glasses" along the way. The key is to be with a company or a team that encourages you to move faster but also helps you clean up if you make a mess. He was fortunate to be with such a company and have tremendous managers, mentors, and guides along the way.

He stared at the framed quote hanging on his office wall.

If you always do what you've always done, you'll always be what you've always been.

It was his mantra, a variation of a quote he'd seen many times before but not exactly those words. He made it his own. Something he'd been doing for 12 years.

At home. At work. Make it your own.

So, here he was, in his beautiful office with panoramic views of the city, waiting for other people to decide his future. He looked at the framed pictures that lined the top of his cabinets and bookshelves. Pictures of his family on vacations, in their new home, sporting events, and at all the milestones in their lives. A picture of himself and Jen when she closed her first big deal, after she found her own purpose in commercial real estate.

He stared down at the picture of himself, younger, behind the bar at Crossroads. It was a picture he'd kept in full view on his desk since the beginning, a signature story he loved to tell, for anyone willing to ask. "How did you get from there to here?" It was a story that defined him. A signature story.

He read the TIP again.

> **What's in Your TIP Jar?**
>
> If it's overflowing with tips and you gave everything you could, then luck and well wishes aren't necessary. Take pride in who you are, the way you communicate, your actions, and the unique value you bring every day. Remember all the people you have helped along the way. Whatever happens today is part of the plan.

The greatest gift you can give to someone is to believe in them, even before they believe in themselves. Jack did that for him so many years ago, and he vowed to pay it forward every chance he could.

It didn't matter if he got the CEO job or not. He wanted it, of course, but if they felt he was too young, or too inexperienced, that would be their decision. It wouldn't affect the way he would move forward because the title would never define him. He'd keep filling the jar until the next opportunity came along. Life is like that. Crossroads everywhere.

The board of directors was meeting, and a decision would be made that day. He had been interviewed a number of times by a number of people. All asked him about his past and his vision for the future, trying to imagine him in the role before he had the role. Just another audition.

The call would come in the afternoon. He would be summoned to the board room. One way or another, his career and his life would move forward because he knew the letters CEO weren't the three letters that would define him. It was WOW that got him here, and it would be WOW that would always keep him focused on his purpose and what truly mattered in his work and his life. His brand was WOW, and he made sure everyone knew it.

22 Good Choices

The kids all got home from their sports and after-school activities, and dinner started promptly at 7:30 p.m. They had a rule for the table. No cell phones. Even him. Whatever it was, and whoever it was, would be able to wait half an hour.

Amazing how the world changed so quickly once everyone had a super computer in their pocket. The ability to talk to the world anytime, anywhere. Instant gratification.

"I want to thank you all for making time to be here. As you know, I was up for a promotion today."

The kids continued to eat.

"And, I'm happy to report that as a team, we're still undefeated. I got the job."

The kids cheered just loud enough to frighten the dog, who started barking.

"Was it close?" Drew asked. "Like, if it was a race, how much did you win by?"

Brian thought for a moment. He could say it wasn't close, but that wouldn't be entirely true. This was actually a chance for a teachable moment.

"If it was a race," Brian answered, "I would have won on a false start."

"What do you mean?" Sara asked.

Brian explained to everyone that the board of directors had brought him into the conference room to let him know their decision to make him the CEO. After all the congratulations, they sat him down and talked about why he was chosen. But they also explained that his lack of experience was a concern for some of the members. Many were leaning towards the head of global operations, who had more than 10 years seniority on Brian. However, as part of the process in being vetted for the role, the company did a very thorough inquiry into all of the candidates, and when they started to probe deeper into this person's background, they found out that his personal life and his personal brand were inconsistent with the person he claimed to be at work. Even though he accomplished great things, he wasn't someone who could represent the company brand, and he was disqualified. Even worse, based on the findings, he was asked to resign.

"He didn't make good choices," Kyra said.

Brian looked over at Jen and gave her a "maybe they do actually listen to us when we talk" smile.

Make good choices. That was something Jen had preached to the kids from the first day they could go off to school on their own. She couldn't be with them and couldn't keep watch over them, so her mantra for them was "make good choices."

Kyra was right. The front-runner for the CEO job didn't make good choices and it caught up with him. Once your words or actions are recorded, as we all know, they can be replayed forever.

"Your mom and I have talked about this topic many times. It may not affect you today, but it certainly will tomorrow. So, before you do anything, you have to ask yourself if your choice represents the best version of you. There is no separation between private and public anymore. Whether you like it or not, you have to assume that everyone is watching, recording, and sharing. What you do today will affect you tomorrow," Brian said.

As the kids were growing up, and technology advanced, he and Jen tried to teach them that managing a consistent brand was harder than ever. Every picture they posted, every word they wrote, and every video recorded—all had the potential to increase or decrease the value of their brands. He could remember numerous times where he would have to tell the kids to take down a picture or a post, explaining to them that the intention of the communication is not always the way it's received in the world. The intention was never meant to be mean, but that doesn't matter when someone else perceives it that way.

They reminded the kids that who you associate with also plays a role in the way you are perceived in the world. Even if you're not sharing and recording everything, someone in your group might be. All it takes is one questionable communication or action to lose everything you've worked so hard for.

Brian always shared stories with the kids when he saw high school athletes lose college scholarships for inappropriate tweets, or when employees of companies lost jobs due to off-brand actions captured on a phone by a customer and then shared with the world. Brian even had to fire a salesperson once because of disparaging comments about clients made during a recorded conference call with those clients, when the salesperson thought the phone was on mute. The lesson? Words matter, and you are never not a representative of your company, your team, or your family.

Brian actually felt sorry for anyone growing up these days, that this was the way of the world. Every mistake or misstep is recorded and archived forever. Words or actions that don't align with a perceived reputation are called out immediately. There is no way to hide. But, on the plus side, for those who do live a consistent life based on consistent beliefs, it was easier than ever to be noticed for the good things they did, and be promoted quicker than ever when they become industry or company famous.

Everyone acknowledged yet another lesson from dad and told Brian how proud they were of him, even though, in reality, he was the second choice and only got the job because the other guy disqualified himself.

Nothing like your kids to keep you grounded.

But it didn't matter. Just hearing the words, "Proud of you, Dad" was all he could ask for. He knew they would truly appreciate his accomplishments later in life, when they had careers and families of their own. Only then would they know how hard he worked to rebrand himself and make the most of every opportunity. As he looked at his family, thinking about the path he was on 12 years ago, and where they were all now, he took a brief moment to be proud of himself.

He thanked everyone again for making the time to be there for dinner and released them to do the dishes and check their cell phones.

Later that evening, after the kids were in their rooms doing homework or on the phone with friends, he and Jen were able to have a moment alone.

"Second choice . . . ," he laughed.

"I did tell you that I loved you, but wasn't sure about them," she added.

"You did say that."

"So, tell me how it really happened," she said. "Don't tell me why they didn't pick the other person. Tell me why they picked you."

Brian sat on the kitchen counter stool and took a sip of water.

"Brand drives business," he said. "That was the phrase they used when they told me why I was the right person for the role."

"I like it," she said. "What does it mean?"

"It means that when you stay true to the brand, the business follows. Business doesn't drive a brand. Brand drives business. Most of the other people up for the role talked a lot about how doing certain things and innovating in certain ways would drive more business and greater revenue and increase the visibility and value of the brand. Outside-in thinking.

"But, I was the only one who had a different point of view. I told them that we needed to focus on brand first. From the ground up, and the inside out. Business doesn't drive anything. People do. People are both the business and the brand. If we focus on developing and aligning individual, team, regional, and global brands we will create one powerful brand that stands for the same things our customers want. That will eventually create more business."

"Brand first," she added.

"Yes. And then they retold my story."

"Which story?"

"My defining moment. Of how I was fired for being average and used that as a jumping off point to start over. Bartending. TIP. WOW. All of it."

"It is a good story," she said.

"They said anyone who could start over, the way I did, and be in the running for this job in such a short time, has the vision and passion to take our expanding company to another level. Brand consistency would be the key to our growth. One consistent brand will drive the business. Oh, and they said they really liked my blue tie."

"Told you." She laughed.

She picked him all those years ago, and he made a promise not to let her down. He was her first choice, and she was his. They were a team through all the ups and downs, aligned in their purpose.

"Thank you," he said, "for not giving up on me."

He kissed her.

"Thank you," she said, "for not giving up on yourself."

She paused.

"So, do you want to do that thing now?" she asked.

"We can always do it tomorrow," he said.

"We can, but we won't," she responded.

"Start a task. Finish a task," he said as he grabbed the keys.

23 Give More, Get More

The place looked the same as always. Even smelled the same.

It had been about two years since he had last been at Crossroads, but every time he walked in, it was as though he'd never left. It was midweek. He knew the place would be quiet enough to do what needed to be done.

There was a small brunette behind the bar that looked like Kelly, but it wasn't her. Kelly quit bartending about six years before. She reached her ultimate goal and finally got that hit TV show, a highly rated, highly watched police drama now in its sixth season. She won an Emmy for playing, what else, a tough cop with a family that owns a bar. His kids watched it all the time. Love the fact that their dad knows a TV star. She still comes back every now and then to the bar and brings all her actor friends with her whenever she's in town.

"Is Jack here?" he asked the brunette, as she was wiping down bottles.

"He's in the office," she responded. "Should be back in a moment."

Brian nodded.

"Can I get you anything while you wait?"

Brian looked at Jen to see if she wanted anything. She shook her head.

"No thanks," he said. "Well, actually, can I see your tip bucket?"

She gave him a quizzical look.

"Not the full one. The empty one at the waitress station." Brian smiled. "It's kind of a surprise for Jack."

She went to the back of the bar and grabbed the metal bucket. She came back and handed it to him.

"Thank you," he said as he put the bucket onto the bar.

Just then, Jack emerged from the back room and spotted Brian.

"So?!" he shouted from across the bar, making New Kelly and the remaining customers jump.

Brian nodded. "I got it!"

"You got it!"

"I got it."

"They wanted the WOW Man?!?!"

"Yeah, we never did find a better name, did we? Still kind of dorky."

"Very dorky," Jen added.

Jack ran up and gave Brian a big bear hug.

"Incredible," Jack said. "Just incredible for the both of you."

Brian smiled.

"We can't stay long, but we had to come in, since it's tradition to come back here after our big moments. Also, we're here for another reason. We wanted to share something with you," Brian said, very seriously.

"Okay? You dying?" Jack asked.

Brian laughed. "No. Actually living. Living quite well."

"We owe much of that to you, Jack," Jen interjected.

"You once told me that a TIP is the result of the effort you put into anything you do. Right?" Brian asked.

Jack nodded. "Sounds like something I'd say."

"I remember when I came in here for my first shift, and you told me that you left the corporate world and opened your own bar because you wanted to stand for something you could be proud of. Remember?"

"I do."

"And you said you borrowed from whomever you could to buy the bar and didn't expect to own it outright for a long time. You said you weren't in it to get rich. It's been 12 years. How much longer do you have to go to pay everything off?"

"If the crowds keep coming in, I'd say at this rate we've got another five or six years to go. The lease is up in three years, though. I've seen the big box chains come in and take over many of the street corners around the neighborhood. Hopefully the building owners decide to renew, otherwise I'll have to look at starting over at another location."

"Jack?"

"Yeah, Brian?"

"The building owner is going to renew."

"And you know this because . . . ?" Jack asked.

". . . because we bought the building," Jen finished.

Jack's jaw dropped.

"Oh, and all your investors and the bank . . . ," Brian continued.

"Yeah?"

"You don't owe them anymore. All debts are paid, and all investors have been bought out."

Brian put a folder full of papers into the metal tip bucket and slid it over to Jack.

"I can't own a bar due to my position in my company, so we've signed all of the documents over to you. The bar is all yours now and will always be all yours," Brian said.

He pulled a dollar bill out of his wallet and slid it across to Jack. On the back of the bill, written in black magic marker were the words "Take It Personally."

It was Jack's same dollar bill from 12 years before.

"I've been hanging onto this for a while," Brian smiled. "You can add it to next month's rent."

Jack shook his head in disbelief.

Brian continued. "This place, and you, changed everything for me and my family."

"For that, we will be forever grateful," Jen added.

"So, consider all of it a big TIP," Brian said.

Jack's eyes welled up. "I don't know what to say. I can never repay this."

"That's the thing. You already have," Brian assured him. "More than you know."

There was a long pause as Jack thought of what he would say next.

"Well," he finally broke the silence, "since you are now my landlord, can I at least buy you both a celebratory drink?"

Brian explained that they would love to stay but had to get back to the house and the kids. Brian also had to get ready for the next day since the company would make the announcement and he was sure to get media inquiries. They assured Jack that they would be back at the end of the week to celebrate properly.

"Wait a minute," Jack said.

He then called to New Kelly and asked her to throw him a couple of the Crossroads T-shirts from the cabinet under the register. He handed the shirts to Brian and Jen.

"Dry-fit. Much better quality than what we used to wear," Jack smiled.

Brian held the shirt up and immediately remembered that night when he put his first Crossroads T-shirt on and how nervous he was to start something new.

Jack walked over and put his arms around Jen and Brian and pulled both of them in for a goodbye group hug.

"Get home safe," he said, "and I better see you both here this weekend. We have a lot to celebrate."

Brian and Jen exited the bar, and as they were about to start walking down the block towards their car, Brian stopped and held up the black T-shirt with the stylistic typeface spelling CROSSROADS across the front. On the back was a drawing of a man and a woman standing at an intersection with their hands on their hips looking up at a road sign with arrows pointing in different directions.

Jen held up her own shirt, looking at the same image.

"That was fun," she said.

"It was," Brian smiled.

She again looked at the shirt.

"You ready for tomorrow?" she asked.

"Yes." He paused and then took a deep breath. "It's going to be more responsibility," he said.

"Always is," she responded.

"More travel," he added.

"Get those miles," she said. "We've got colleges to visit for the next eight years."

He laughed as he put his arm around her, and they began walking down the block to the car.

"I'm thinking maybe the green tie for tomorrow," he said. "Or the blue. What do you think?"

She paused. "I think I love you."

He stopped and kissed her. That was the only thing that really mattered: the love and respect of his most important customer.

They got to the car, and he opened the passenger side door for his wife. As he walked around the back of the car to the driver's side, he took one last look at the blue and red CROSSROADS sign down the block. He would definitely be back, but now it was time to get home and get some sleep. Tomorrow would be a very big day.

The end, and a new beginning.

TWENTY TAKEAWAY TIPS
FOR SUCCESS

There were a lot of messages packed into one simple story. For your convenience, here are 20 Takeaway TIPs to remind you of the keys to success, as you continue your own journey towards a stronger personal brand, greater personal accountability, and lasting success.

1. You are the only person accountable for your success or failure.

2. If you don't know your brand, others will attempt to define it for you.

3. You are being labeled at every moment of every day.

4. Don't be a Justa.

5. Unique value is being known for one thing that only you can bring.

6. No one will hire you, keep you, or promote you if you don't add value.

7. Every day is an audition to keep the job you have or get the job you want.

8. Make your manager's job easier.

9. Start a task. Finish a task.

10. A stand-out performer will always have more value than a stand-in.

11. Embrace conflict and crisis. That's when people of value are needed most.

12. Make commitments, not decisions.

13. You are never not a representative of your company or team brand.

14. Your signature story will tell who you are, what you stand for, and who you help.

15. Consistency of beliefs, words, and actions is the key to your reputation and success.

16. Return on action (ROA) is the measurement of the commitment and investment you make in yourself.

17. Create WOW experiences for customers and colleagues.

18. People will sponsor you only if you add value to *their* business and *their* brand.

19. Lasting success is the result of making good choices at a series of crossroads in work and life.

20. Give all you can. Help people be their best. You will be rewarded in return.

For a downloadable PDF of this list, and other TIPs and resources, visit davegordon.net.

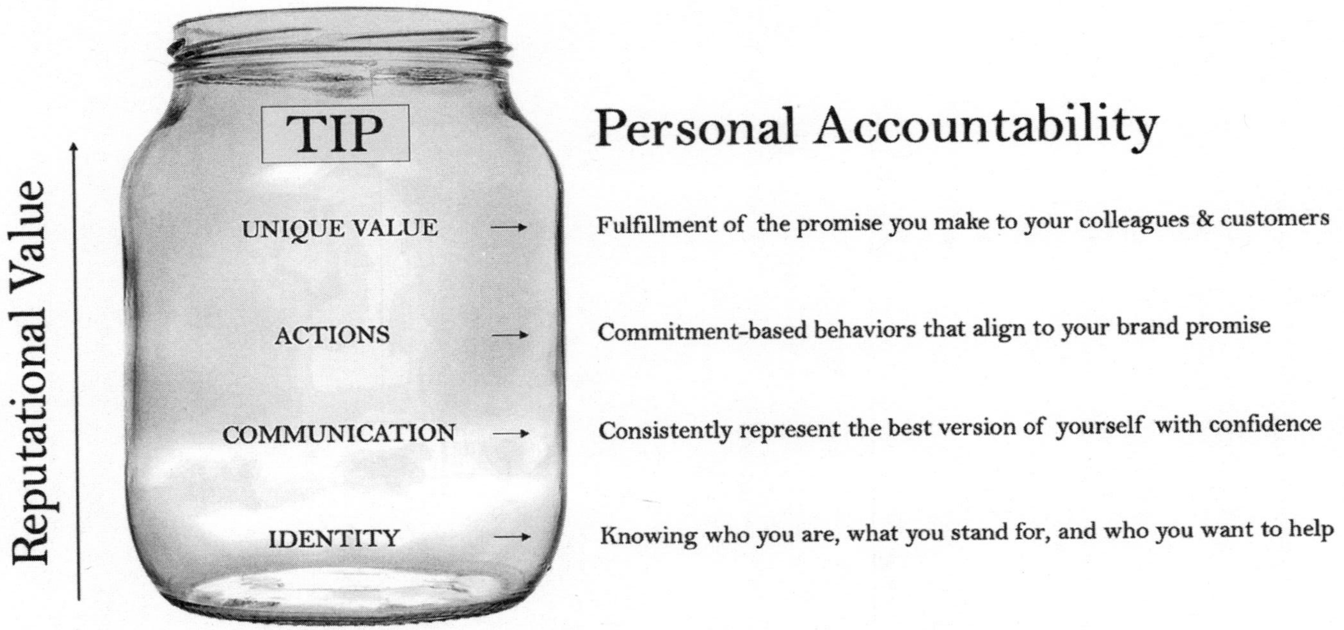

Personal Accountability

Fulfillment of the promise you make to your colleagues & customers

Commitment-based behaviors that align to your brand promise

Consistently represent the best version of yourself with confidence

Knowing who you are, what you stand for, and who you want to help

TIP

UNIQUE VALUE

ACTIONS

COMMUNICATION

IDENTITY

Reputational Value

To download a printable PDF of the TIP Personal Accountability Model please visit davegordon.net

Figure A.1 The Personal Accountability TIP Model

PERSONAL ACCOUNTABILITY MODEL AND ACTION PLAN

Personal accountability is being responsible for the success or consequences that are the result of the beliefs, words, and actions within your control. As you read in the story, Brian only achieved the results and recognition he wanted when he held himself accountable for his results and his reputation. He filled his tip jar from the bottom up, by first understanding who he was, and then communicating his aspirational brand of WOW in every communication and action. He provided unique value in every interaction and ultimately rose through his organization to the top spot in a short time because he was outperforming everyone else.

Brian's story can be your story in any industry and any career. I know because I have been helping people identify, communicate, and deliver their unique value to build stronger personal brands for many years through my coaching, training, and inspirational keynote presentations for teams and companies of all sizes.

The personal accountability model shown in Figure A.1 is simple. It shows you the areas in need of consistency that make up your overall reputational value. If you take the time to master them, you will live a more authentic, accountable, and aspirational life.

Since I am not with you to motivate or coach you in person, I'd like to take you through a journey, similar to the one Brian took in the story, to become the best version of yourself. It is a journey of personal accountability, high performance, and lasting success. But you have to be willing to do the work.

It's very easy to tell someone else who they are, but much harder to look at yourself. Whether you are just starting your career, aspiring to the next level, or still want to make a difference as you think about other endeavors, you are never too young or too old to build a stronger personal brand. So, let's start with some thought-provoking questions.

Identity

- List your unique talents.
- What do others say you are the best at doing?
- How would people describe you, today, in one word? (your label)
- Is that label how you want to be perceived?
- If not, what is your aspirational brand? (one word)
- What tasks put you in a state of flow?
- What motivates you, beyond money?
- If your brand had a tagline like Nike's "Just do it," what would it be?

- Describe a moment in your life when you overcame adversity to bounce back from a challenge in your life or career? (signature story)

- Describe a time when you were your most confident, strongest, and ready to take on the world. When were you a "fierce bear?"

- Who do you want to help? Why?

After answering these questions, you should be able to get a clear picture of how you see yourself. If you aren't happy with the picture, that's okay. We are here to identify gaps that can be improved and create the foundation of a more accountable personal brand.

Communication

- How do you normally make an entrance? Your energy? Attitude?

- What do you believe other people think about you as you enter a room?

- What is the promise or problem your brand communicates?

- How do you create an experience for others with your words?

- How do you make people feel?

- Do your communications create conflict or collaboration? Explain.

- Does your verbal and nonverbal language represent your aspirational brand?

- In what ways do you "bring it" at your job? In your life?

- How do you educate people about the value you can bring to their world?

- If you were invited back to be the graduation speaker at your former high school or college, what would your speech be about? What advice would you give to the graduating class?

After answering these questions, you should be able to get a clear picture of how you communicate your personal brand. Remember, if you're not excited about your words and your communication, how can you expect the person on the other end of the communication to be excited about you? The goal in this section is to be aware that your words and nonverbal language are the only things other people have to judge whether you offer a promise or a problem.

Actions

- How do you invest in yourself? Take stock of your actions and behaviors in your work and life and categorize them into proactive, reactive, distractive, or destructive.

- Looking at the distractive or destructive actions to your aspirational brand, which will you stop, and which will you replace with proactive choices?

- What will the return on action (ROA) be for each new investment of your time?

- Define what consistency means to you in your life and career.

- What are the excuses you make for not giving 100% of yourself to your career and your life?

- How would you react if a bottle of red wine spilled at the table? How would members of your team react?

- What book or movie character do you most resemble in a crisis?

- Give an example when you gave more without thinking of the rewards, and ultimately received more than you expected in return?

- List the new people, new experiences, and new learnings you have encountered in the past year. What differences have they made in your life or career?

- List the tasks you start but don't finish.

- List the tasks you start and always finish.

- On a scale of 1–100, how personally accountable are you for your actions and your reputation?

- What are you going to do to make it 100?

- When did you last protect the brand of your team or company? How?

Personal branding is the process of applying branding principles to human behaviors to create consistency of experience and results. Human behavior is inconsistent. But following a guideline of consistency will ensure that people trust you and want you because you always deliver results consistent with your promise.

Unique Value

- What is the mission of your team?

- What value do you bring to your team?

- How do you make your boss's job easier?

- Pick one person in your life who believes you are valuable to them. Why? What value do you bring? Can you see the world from their eyes?

- Do people know who you help and why you help them?

- What results are you most proud of?

- What is your greatest success? Who knows about it?

- Fill in the blank. I am an expert at _____.

- Are you a stand-in or stand-out? Explain.

- List all the people you believe would recommend you for a position in their company or on their team, effectively putting their own reputations on the line by recommending you? Who would sponsor your brand?

- How do you create WOW in your work and life?

- If you had achieved all the success you ever wanted, who would you thank? What did they do for you to deserve that thanks? How would you thank them?

At the beginning of the story, Brian didn't feel valuable to anyone. As he began to feel good about himself, his job, and the value he was bringing to his customers, he gave more. The key to adding unique value is to know your strengths and give the very best of yourself. You are valuable to someone, most likely to many people. The key is to give everything you have. When your goal is to create a WOW experience for your colleagues and customers, you will be perceived as having unique value. When that happens, your story starts getting told even when you're not in the room.

Creating a Brand Advisory Group

Now that you have taken the time to get to know yourself, it's important to know how you are being perceived by your colleagues and customers. Your reputation is not what you say about yourself; it's what others say about you. Remember that intention and perception are two very different things. To find out if your intended personal brand is your actual reputation, it will take a bit of focus and a focus group.

Pick between seven and nine people from areas of your personal and professional life who interact with you on a consistent basis. Create your own brand advisory group. Ask them the following questions:

1. How would you describe my personal brand in one word?

2. How does my brand make you feel?

3. What do you hear *other* people say about my brand?

4. How is my brand unique?

5. Does my brand convey a promise or a problem? Please describe.

6. How could I be more valuable to you?

You can send them the questions to answer on their own or have an in-person discussion, depending on what is most comfortable. The answers are meant to determine if your brand is strong, weak, consistent, or inconsistent. Remember, you are not asking people to judge you, the person. You are asking for feedback on your brand, your reputation. They should not be judging you. They should be letting you know how you make people feel and the value you bring.

After you ask the questions, accept the answers without argument or defensiveness. You must remember that your reputation is formed by everything in your TIP jar. It is who you are, what you stand for, how you communicate, the actions you choose, and the unique value you provide. It is all of that which determines how you are actually remembered in the minds of your customers. Once you get your answers, acknowledge whether your intended brand is being conveyed and whether you are making the most out of your life and career. Are you focused on your strengths and on what makes you happy, or are you destined for a life of average?

When you get the answers, take a look and see if they align with how you see yourself. If there are inconsistencies, you know you have some work to do. If they are aligned, then you are consistent in your words and actions.

*   *   *

After answering all of the personal questions and running your own focus group, you should be better prepared to hold yourself accountable for the reputation, results, and recognition you receive in your work and life.

If you are willing to do the work and commit to taking accountability for your future, you will achieve the lasting success you want.

This is a small book and a simple story designed to make you think about yourself and your future in a proactive and empowering way. I hope after reading the story, answering the questions, and listening to your focus group you will have enough information to find or keep a career that fulfills you.

Before you close this book please answer the following three questions. If you know the answers and can consistently repeat them, no matter who asks, you are ahead of most people in your industry and are destined to be a stand-out in everything you do.

What is your aspirational brand, in one word?

Does that word launch you out of bed in the morning and put you to sleep at night? Does it express what you want to be known for? If not, you have the wrong word.

What is your purpose statement? It begins with "I help people..."

If you have your word and your purpose, your title won't matter. You will know why you are here and who you are supposed to help.

What is your signature story of results and success?

When you have your story, it's easy to tell and retell. If it's a great story, people will tell it for you, even when you're not around.

I hope the story of TIP, and the action plan, inspires you to give more in your work and life. It is a simple strategy, but it's the execution of that strategy most people find difficult. Stay on track. Stay on brand. And, most of all, stay true to the very best version of yourself.

Take It Personally,
Dave Gordon

For more information about me and my work, or to inquire about my availability to speak at your next meeting or event, please reach out:

E-mail: dave@gordoncc.com

Twitter: @davegordon_9

Instagram: @davegordon_9

LinkedIn: linkedin.com/in/davegordon9

Or, visit my website at www.davegordon.net where you can get all the information you need and sign up for my newsletter.

Resources

Please visit **www.davegordon.net** for tips, tools, guides and other useful resources to help create:

- Inspiring Leaders
- High Performing Teams
- Loyal Customers
- Stronger Brands

Please contact John Wiley & Sons at (877) 762-2974 for bulk orders if you are interested in purchasing *TIP* for:

- Large group events
- National and international sales meetings
- Leadership conferences
- Industry and association conferences
- Intern programs and new hire onboarding
- Leadership and high potential programs
- Organizational and brand alignment initiatives
- Large-scale team building and motivation